GW00537285

D.I.Y. DETENTE

D.I.Y. DETENTE

A Guide to Meeting People in the Soviet Union

Edited by Ann Pettitt
Co-edited by Linnie Baldwin

QUARTET BOOKS

LONDON   NEW YORK

First published by Quartet Books Limited 1987
A member of the Namara Group
27/29 Goodge Street, London W1P 1FD

Copyright © Ann Pettitt 1987

British Library Cataloguing in Publication Data
The D.I.Y. détente book.
   1. Soviet Union – Handbooks, manuals, etc.
   I. Pettitt, Ann
   914.7'04854   DK40

ISBN 0-7043-2606-X

Printed in Great Britain by
The Camelot Press Limited, Southampton

Acknowledgements

Compiling, editing and writing this book had to be fitted in to a life as complicated as that of any middle-aged woman with young children who wants to be everything and do everything, and so I could not possibly have managed it on my own. I am particularly indebted to Linnie Baldwin without whose persistent cheerful encouragement and many hours of practical help, this book would have foundered at the second-bottle-of-wine stage. She shared all the hard work of creating this book out of nothing, when we had no prospects of a publisher. I owe thanks to Jean McCollister for intelligent appraisal of the text, to Stephen Shenfield, Jeff Gleisner and Cathy Fitzpatrick for helpful and informed suggestions and for filling out my own scant knowledge of Soviet society; to Barbara Bonczyk for generously typing when no money was available, and to my partner Barry Wade for practical support while I worked, for faith in the outcome, and for reading the first draft and being a good critic; to Women For Life on Earth Russia Trip fund, and all those who contributed to it, and to Karman Cutler for a piece of neat investment thereof, which supplied the small but vital sum of money which enabled the book to be started; to Jennifer Bradshaw and Linda Brandon at Quartet for helping me to clarify the writing and arrange this hotch-potch into some sort of sensible order; and to all the contributors for so generously giving their time, and for their encouragement and optimism.

CONTENTS

Part Two: BRIEF ENCOUNTERS, FRIENDS
AND LOVERS

Part Three: TOURLANDZIA AND BEYOND

Appendices

Ann Pettitt
Introduction

'In a way, we were in the Myth Demolition business' – Caroline
Westgate

The purpose of this book is to place a useful tool in the hands of
people from 'the West' who want to visit the USSR and meet
Russian people. It is not exactly a guide-book – these already
exist and their virtues and shortcomings are considered in our
section on 'useful books'. It is rather a briefing for beginners
written by beginners, on how to survive within a territory as
much psychological as geographical: that which lies outside
'Tourlandzia', the areas set aside for use by foreigners.

The information and personal experiences offered in this
book are drawn from a variety of sources, some Russian, some
American, but mostly from British women who visited the
Soviet Union between 1983 and 1985. Since that time Mikhail
Gorbachev has consolidated his power and begun his programme of 'perestroika' – meaning reconstruction. Some of his
reforms are far-reaching and indicate a determination to break
the mould of the Brezhnev era in which Soviet life congealed
and stagnated. The increasing flow of ideas within the country,
and the new policy of 'glasnost' (openness) within the press
leading to the possibility of honest discussion of problems, and

the sense of change taking place – all make the USSR a more exciting and challenging place to visit now than at any other time since the first years of the revolution.

All our contributors, and all who have helped with the production, have done so because they believe that the barriers preventing contact between the ordinary people of 'East' and 'West' support the 'Cold War' waged by both sides and so contribute significantly to a situation which threatens human, possibly even planetary, survival. Their aim has been to break down these barriers in small, personal ways, some of which are real and some, imaginary.

This book, therefore, is a small contribution which we hope will prove useful to a growing movement taking place on both sides of the Iron Curtain. Such a movement might be called 'Do-It-Yourself-Détente'.

We need to make some things clear at the outset. First of all, a word about that curious phrase 'the Iron Curtain'. It has been pointed out that this phrase is itself of Cold War origin, coined by Winston Churchill in order to instil anti-Soviet feelings in a post-war, European population, still under the impression that Russia was our ally. That may be so, but I don't think Churchill invented the Iron Curtain. Some people believe that it was a figment of Winston's imagination and that the phrase should not be used, because of its origins. There can be no doubt, however, that an elaborate system of psychological barriers and taboos, a system of tacitly understood 'rules', *does* exist and that such a system is designed to prevent normal relationships between the peoples of East and West. We use the phrase 'Iron Curtain' therefore, as a shorthand to describe these barriers and the fears they provoke. Every story in this book engages in some way with the Iron Curtain dilemma.

The wide-ranging contributions to *D.I.Y. Détente* are intended to promote the kind of travel, by individuals and small groups, that can lead to a better understanding of a strange land and to the development of genuine friendships with its inhabitants. We are well aware that in trying to describe honestly the obstacles a visitor with this kind of aim may encounter, we may seem to be confirming traditional Western prejudices about the Soviet Union. 'I'd come to the Soviet Union to *explode* myths like these,' exclaims the writer of our first story in dismay, when her new-found Soviet friend warns her of the possibility of KGB 'listeners' to their conversations.

But we cannot tailor the truth of experience to fit the way we would like it to be: if the reality is more complex, and more of a problem than we realised, that is all the more reason for plain speaking and honesty. Both Russians and Westerners have fears about meeting each other and telling each other what they really think. 'I've always wanted to go to Russia, but I've never dared,' said my Health Visitor. She followed it up with: 'But tell me, if you go, can you really meet Russians, see how they live – aren't you kept apart?' 'Ah well,' I said, 'that's what this book's about.'

The Iron Curtain won't go away because we wish it away. It will only weaken by being criss-crossed innumerable times, until there are so many holes it has become see-through. This brings me to a second important point. When it comes to crossing that East–West frontier, we are talking about a largely one-way traffic. If you go to Russia and make friends, you won't, under present circumstances (unless there are near-miraculous changes in the Soviet State system) be able to invite your friends back to stay with you for a few weeks, to get a truthful, warts-and-all look at the myth-populated 'West'. Travel to the West is limited to specially invited groups, and is a tremendous 'treat'. As such, it is granted as a reward by the State for 'good', conformist behaviour. Most Soviet citizens one meets take it for granted that their view of Florence, Paris, London or New York will never go beyond the picture-postcard. However startling some of the changes taking place within the USSR, however much 'freer' the atmosphere, there is no indication that the leadership is ready to make travel to the West a simple matter of money.

The restrictions on travel abroad that confine the vast majority of Soviet citizens within their own country do not, however, dim their curiosity, nor poison with suspicion their desire for friendship and contact with Westerners. On the contrary, the travellers who have given us accounts of their experiences have all remarked on the genuine warmth and welcome given those invited into homes, and the surprising ease with which contacts may be made at random, some leading to lasting friendships carried on in spite of the difficulties.

This is one of many paradoxes explored in the book: we, who can satisfy our curiosity about 'them' simply by saving up the modest sum required for a package holiday, are blasé about our freedom and often ignore its possibilities – while they, who cannot hop on a plane to see us, demonstrate (particularly among the young) a heightened, in many cases quite obsessive, curiosity about the West. Nevertheless the traffic from the West is increasing and more and more people are overcoming their fears and discovering that booking a Russian package holiday is as simple as booking any trip abroad. Since the Chernobyl explosion, a new fear of radioactive contamination has arisen. For the majority of visitors who stay in Moscow or Leningrad this should prove no deterrent (see Post Chernobyl Postscript). Sadly, however, few visitors discover for themselves the answer to my Health Visitor's second question.

There are two ways most people travel to the Soviet Union. They go as 'tourists', usually staying full board in Intourist hotels in the main cities, or they go as a 'delegation' by arrangement with one of the many Soviet State committees or Party organisations, such as the Komsomol.* Either way, it is quite possible to spend your entire visit without meeting a single person beyond those 'appointed' to meet you: your guides and interpreters, the 'floor-ladies', the hotel staff, the members of your host organisation and the people invited by them to meet you.

This is not to say that the people you will meet in the normal course of a tourist trip or a delegation are *all* Communist Party members, or KGB informers, or any other product of an outsider's paranoid view of a one-Party state. However since, to some degree, meeting Westerners is part of their job, the experience of meeting Russians for whom this is not so is so rewarding that it is well worth the extra resourcefulness that

*Youth section of the Communist Party of the USSR.

may be needed to place oneself in their path. I am talking about stratagems as simple as using public transport instead of the coach provided, skipping some organised group excursions in favour of random wanderings on foot alone or with a friend, eating in public cafeterias instead of always at the hotel, or queueing up for goods in the Russian shops instead of using the hard-currency 'Beriozka' shop in the hotel.

All these ways of mingling with and savouring at least a little of ordinary Russian life may seem straightforward, but most people do not do this, believing that because a 'programme' of tours and visits for each day and some evenings is provided with coach transport, deviation from this 'programme' will produce unforeseen consequences, leading to retribution of some kind. However, the message from those of our contributors who spent part, and in some cases all, of their time skipping the pre-arranged schedule in favour of their own inclinations is quite clear: nobody can stop you or indeed seriously attempt to do so, and while some guides plainly disapprove of 'deviationists', others are delighted to have some charges who need less nannying and are prepared to look after themselves.

Just as no visitor can hope to avoid meeting the Iron Curtain in some form or other, so no visitor to the Soviet Union can avoid the issue of war and peace. Not only are there slogans everywhere on the theme of Peace – and often Friendship – but the topic is frequently raised by people you meet. Often their attitudes show an uncanny symmetry with those popularly held in the West. 'Our Soviet bombs are for peace only', I remember one old lady fervently declaring in the course of a discussion which arose in a hotel kitchen.

The Soviet State goes to considerable lengths to impress its peaceful intentions upon both its own citizens and those from other countries. In fact, a particular department called 'the Peace Committee', with branches in the main cities, exists to implement what they sometimes describe as 'the Peace Offensive'. The Peace Committees receive foreign visitors, host delegations and organise large rallies, sometimes timed to coincide with those held in the West. The slogans and speeches at such gatherings never implicate the Soviet Union in the arms

escalation. The Western governments are, of course, to blame –
their need to arm themselves is seen as spurious.

On the other hand, even the most casual visitor will be
frequently reminded of the Soviet sacrifices during World War
Two. The loss of twenty million people and the ruin of countless
towns and villages is always presented as evidence for two
things: the need for a strong military force as the only way to
avert the possibility of another invasion; and the depth of the
Soviet people's desire to avoid war, having already suffered so
much. Taken together, they form a formidable but familiar
argument: Peace through Strength – the motto of NATO. The
visitor who previously did not give much thought to this sort of
thing is likely to be stimulated to give it more consideration
afterwards. Particularly in cases where personal friendships are
established with Soviet people, the effect is to strengthen and
deepen the desire for a new East–West relationship which is not
based on precarious military competition.

To widen one's experience requires a little confidence, a little
language or at least some useful Russian phrases (though even
this is not absolutely essential as more often that not an
informal guide will materialise for the most incompetent
Westerner, lost on the Metro or in the street), good walking
shoes, some 'tokens of friendship' to exchange as gifts, and
above all the creative ability to welcome the unexpected.

The question which interrupts this enthusiastic flow, and
which everyone asks as soon as you begin to talk about meeting
ordinary Russians: 'Will I be followed if I leave the main tourist
areas, and will I bring Russians I meet with into danger?' will be
dealt with in subsequent chapters. The point of these remarks is
only to make it plain that if looking at buildings and museums
bores you, there is no law that prevents you discovering the
exciting alternative of shared human experience.

This area is a kind of psychological frontiers-land, and the
'rules' are being made up by the people of the Two Worlds who
venture there. We can't tell you, for certain, what can and can't
be done. We can only tell you our stories of what people have
done, what they've tried and what they couldn't do, in the hope
that others will be encouraged to enlarge, however slightly, the

boundaries of the possible, for all of us.

The importance of creating a stable, lasting peace between East and West cannot be emphasised enough. But when one realises that 'peace' itself can mean different things to different people, the problems that lie in the way appear greater. We seem in fact, to have something of a Gordian knot on our hands. It can all make you feel as if you've stumbled into something rather bigger than you bargained for when you booked a week's package holiday to somewhere a bit different.

And of course, you have. This book is the story of what happened to some of the people who took this risk and who didn't regret it.

Note: The Editor and contributors do know that 'Russian' is but one of many nationalities that make up the Soviet Union. (Most of the encounters here described are in fact with Russians, and where this is not so it is usually made plain.) We have preferred to use the popular, if slightly inaccurate, word 'Russians' rather than 'Soviets' which may be correct but sounds contrived.

PART ONE

D.I.Y. DETENTE

Ann Pettitt
The Russia Trip:
The Story of this Book*

Our story begins in the Towy valley, where Wales looks towards the Atlantic, winter home of the Russian white-fronted goose. For the past five years I have driven up and down that valley, meeting friends and intermittently plotting the downfall of civilisation as we know it. The first year, we plotted a women's march to Greenham Common, which ended in a 'peace-camp' that has inspired women the world over. The next year, we plotted another push-baby plod to some flat buildings on the Pembrokeshire coast called US Brawdy, one of those obscure but vital links in the plans for war. It was a perfect day in June 1982 when we set off on our hot, blistery walk to Brawdy, singing naive and idealistic songs. A few of us stopped off to rest in the village of Maenclochog, and it was here that the next assault was conceived. This became known as 'the Russia Trip'. In fact some credit for the idea should go to the General Public. 'Why don't you go to Russia?' they would shout. 'Why don't we?' we began to think.

The plan was to collect together a group of ordinary, nice, trustworthy women, distinguished only by their concern for the future of our planet and their willingness to act in its defence.

*Part of this text first appeared in *Planet: The Welsh Internationalist*, 1984.

They would go to Russia and there, with the co-operation of the Soviet authorities, they would meet ordinary Russians, communicate through their own interpreters, and thus bring back to their communities a credible picture of Russian people and their lives. We would not seek to replace one myth by another, but would try instead to introduce a ray of truth into the fog of popular ideas about 'the enemy'.

I can with difficulty imagine a world in which the inhabitants of 'East' and 'West' no longer live in fear of each other, but are inspired by a new, global imperative: to find our proper place as careful custodians of our unique, wasted, still-beautiful planet. But to get on with the story. The kitchen table of Karman Cutler (mother, housewife and Trades Union organiser) in Ammanford, West Wales, was the honoured setting for the painstaking process of translating these airy-fairy notions into reality. Two years after the Greenham march, Karman and I were back round the same table, with the same feeling of not knowing where to begin. Only this time it was worse, for the wildly conflicting advice we got from within the peace movement revealed serious differences of opinion of which we had scarcely been aware. Some said that as Greenham originators, we would inevitably be exploited by any Soviet authorities we approached; others seemed to think we wanted to collaborate with them, and most were confident that we would get nowhere without official co-operation.

Then, at an early stage in our investigations into precisely how we, with no money, no Russian language and no contacts, were going to achieve our vague ambition of meeting ordinary Russian people, we were intrigued to hear rumours of the existence of a group of Soviet citizens whose ideas appeared to echo our own. Later we discovered that memorable day in the West Wales village of Maenclochog was also the day that a group of Russians first met in a Moscow flat to launch their own idea of a grass-roots détente. The path they chose was the one we had glimpsed when we too had begun to develop a curiosity about Russians, about their view of our global predicament. If the people of East and West could have contact with one another, if we could meet and exchange uncensored letters; if there could be co-operation in finding solutions to common problems; if research could be shared and schools exchange visits; in short if people, unhindered by their governments, could work on a new East–West relationship – then the Cold War would begin to collapse, and with it the irrational fears that allow governments to pile up defence weapons that defend no one against the real threat of a globally catastrophic war.

A dozen or so people had met in Moscow on June 4 1982 to sign a document called 'An Appeal to the Governments and Publics of the USSR and the USA'. This appeal called for a three-way dialogue across the East–West divide – between people at a personal level, between governments, and between the people and their own governments. No arms agreements can really succeed, they argued, unless a climate of trust is built up by people at all levels. The founders of the 'Group for Trust' did not see themselves as critics of their own state. The point was to escape from the endless stalemate of each side off-loading responsibility onto the other for the common mess. They did not want to add their own voices to the accusatory chorus of the Cold War.

The infant group hoped to make contact with the Scandinavian peace women who, as guests of the Peace Committee, were leading a march through Moscow at the time. But instead they found themselves under house arrest. Shortly afterwards a leading member was sent to a psychiatric hospital. The few notices about the group that appeared in the West attracted little attention. The Soviet journalists who had been invited to that first meeting had known better than to attend.

Suspicion greeted this weird new arrival upon the international peace-keeping scene. Western peace movement sophisticates discerned the hand of the CIA, the KGB, or both. Only a tiny handful of people in the West had made the journey to investigate this group for themselves. One of those people was Jean McCollister, a young American who was studying geography at Oxford on a Rhodes Scholarship. She spoke Russian well, and had been thinking hard about a new kind of East–West détente when she heard about the Group for Trust. She travelled to Moscow and spent a week with them, and returned inspired by their dedication. I met her, by a stroke of luck, just as Karman and I were beginning to feel we were getting nowhere and the whole idea was a bit beyond us. Jean brought with her exactly what was needed – an informed perspective on the USSR that avoided both cynicism and naivety – and together Karman, Jean and I prepared to rush in where angels feared to tread.

Our visit to Moscow in May 1983 was designed as a sort of reconnoitre, the preliminary to a larger visit by about thirty women which we hoped would be effectively publicised. We decided to try to meet both the Group for Trust and the 'official' Soviet Peace Committee (of whom descriptions ranged from 'government stooges' to 'sincere representatives of the mass peace movement of Soviet people') to solicit the co-operation of both for our idea.

We were not, to our relief, met at Moscow airport by the flower-bearing massed ranks of Young Pioneers some had predicted. In fact, we were the only people on the plane who had to queue up with the Russians for transport into the city. When we rang the Peace Committee, we had some difficulty persuading them that we would need a whole afternoon to discuss our proposals and not just the half-hour they offered.

Then we plunged into the grey and ochre city, whose dusty air hung heavy with lilac pollen, in search of the Group for Trust. Eventually we found ourselves in front of a high-rise block of flats. The ground floor door was firmly locked, and we didn't know the code to open it. Never mind – someone had pushed the glass out of the window beside. We scrambled through the hole and up to the eighteenth floor, where in response to our ring a tall, grey-haired man opened the door and literally jumped for joy. We went into the kitchen of Yuri and Olga Medvedkov, and the tea and the talk began to flow as other Group for Trust members, summoned by phone calls and Russian bush telegraph, arrived.

It did not take many hours of fascinating, addictive conversation for us to realise a few things. The first was that these people were motivated by the same hopes and fears as ourselves. They took the threat of the Arms Race seriously enough to make the apparently crazy attempt, as individuals, to intervene in a seemingly inexorable process towards destruction. But it took us a while to convince them that no-one paid us to start a peace-camp, that we had acted on our own initiative as well. They found this hard to believe because 'Greenham Peace Champions' were evidently being officially hailed by the Soviet media for resisting 'Cruise' missiles. But the reporting edited out the spontaneous, home-made essence of the movement. It made it sound wooden and contrived, as if platform speakers mouthed Soviet anti-Americanisms at 'mass rallies' where people sat neatly in rows. We remembered only too well our efforts to have Greenham seriously reported at home, while here we were just part of the muzak, equally unbelievable cardboard 'heroines'.

Finally, it was plain that while our lives could be disrupted as a result of our actions, we were at least able to choose how far this should go – whether or not to live at Greenham, whether to pay a fine or go to jail, for instance. The personal risks these people took were in another league. They scrupulously avoided breaking any Soviet Law. But despite their efforts at optimism and their resolution not to dwell on 'harassments', the State's response in the form of loss of jobs and the sinister threats of the KGB, borne out by a sudden rise in the personal accident rate, was unnerving them. No replies had ever been received to their repeated attempts to communicate with the Peace Committee, which in answer to queries from visiting Westerners such as ourselves, was denying the existence of the Group for Trust. Even an exhibition devoted to showing the suffering of Hiroshima had been broken up by KGB thugs, and they were at a loss to know what to do.

When someone came up with the idea that we should take a member of the Group for Trust along with us to the meeting we had fixed up with the Peace Committee, we agreed. It seemed the only sensible thing to do, for we had to make it unmistakably clear to the State authorities that if we were 'Peace Champions', then so were these people. We could hardly ignore the fact that we were in a position to influence their situation. Such an action obviously carried a high risk of alienating the authorities whose co-operation we were seeking; but on the other hand, how could we fix up a highly public 'Peace and Friendship' trip, without the very people who were making peace through friendship in the personal way we shared, especially when they were being treated so badly.

We spent the next few days talking with both the Group for Trust and, through Jean, with as many other people as we could. We found that 'more personal contact between East and West' was not only what the Group for Trust wanted, but was a favourite theme of many people we encountered, often at random. When the time for the Peace Committee meeting came, Olga Medvedkov was chosen to accompany us. She seemed to think there was very little chance that she would be allowed an inch beyond the door, but as it turned out we were late for our appointment. This was through no fault of our own; our taxi had broken down in the midst of heavy traffic beneath the less than sanguine gaze of Felix Dzerzhinsky, first head of the secret police, whose black, flowerless statue stands in the middle of the square before the KGB headquarters, the Lubyanka. The result was that when we arrived at the large building on Prospekt Mira, we were shown straight up and into the office of Oleg Kharkhardin, vice-chairman of the Peace Committee, by a junior fellow who didn't want to keep his superiors waiting any longer. About eight men and women were standing around, looking nervous. One of them said sharply: 'We were expecting three. Now, you are four.' 'We are "Women for Life on Earth",' I said, wildly. 'We grow every day.'

The next half-hour during which Olga Medvedkov sat with us facing Oleg Kharkhardin and the seven other members of this Soviet State institution, felt like a watershed in our lives. It was as if everything that had gone before had led to this point and everything that happened afterwards would be marked in some way by this episode. Kharkhardin was a broad man with a dome-shaped head and broad-rimmed spectacles. His manner was that of someone used to other people being afraid of him; if he had served his apprenticeship as an interrogator I would not have been surprised. Things would not have been quite the same if we hadn't been sitting in his own office, an honour accorded to us by virtue of our status as 'Greenham heroines'.

As the introductions began he stared at each of us in turn with hard, suspicious eyes. Finally his gaze came to rest upon the pad on which Olga was jotting down names. The handwriting was unmistakably Russian. Noticing this, the other Committee members began to squirm nervously in their seats. Trickles of sweat began to run down my sides. A secretary, heavily made up and wearing jewellery and fashionable Western clothes, minced up and down with cups of tea. I dared not pick up the cup in front of me in case my hand shook; I noticed no one else touched theirs either.

It was Olga's turn to introduce herself. She did so in a clear, crisp voice. She got as far as the word 'doveriye' (trust) and was interrupted. During the three or four sentences she had spoken the fidgeting of the Committee had given way to loud commentary. Some drummed on the table with matchboxes to drown her out, others passed frantic notes down the table, while the interpreter, at a complete loss, nervously scored lines right through his pad. The hubbub instantly subsided as Kharkhardin began a lengthy speech, his eyes carefully excluding Olga as if she did not exist.

'I will not allow her to speak,' he said. 'This is my office. I make the rules; I decide who can speak and who cannot.' He described Olga as an 'element' and contrasted the 'tiny, insignificant minority' who were the Trust Group with the 'true, mass peace movement of the Soviet Union, which has two hundred and forty million members' (in other words, the entire adult population). Hinting that someone had put us up to this 'act of provocation' he accused the Group for Trust of 'stealing the banner of Peace' from the true, patriotic 'Peace Champions'. To this day I believe that Kharkhardin thought the Group for Trust and our involvement in it was nothing other than the work of the CIA.

'Whatever we have to discuss with Madame Medvedkov,' he concluded chillingly, 'it will not be round *this* table. We do not appreciate this initiative of yours, to say the very least. This is an abuse of our hospitality.' We seized on that word to make our point: 'Without women of initiative,' we said, 'there would have been no Greenham Common for the Peace Committee to praise so lavishly. As for hospitality, that's what we have had from the Group for Trust.' Surreptitious grins began to show on the faces of the juniors at the bottom of the table at this unexpectedly lively interchange.

It is true that, but for the presence of Olga, we might not have been so struck by the similarity between this Peace Committee boss and a tank; and so, as plenty of peace-loving folk back here have pointed out, we perhaps unnecessarily created difficulties for ourselves leading to subsequent entanglements with what one person euphemistically described as 'the unfortunate apparatus of the security state'. What for us was a simple act of solidarity, and an effective way of asking questions that would otherwise have been evaded, was regarded not only by the Soviet authorities but by a number of people in our own peace movement, as an unwarranted intervention in Soviet 'internal affairs'. But, because of our 'blunder', we understood certain things in half an hour that it can take years to grasp.

The meeting did not end when Olga, of her own accord, left, followed shortly afterwards by Mr Kharkhardin. We continued for another two hours, trying to explain why the kind of trip we had in mind, with many informal and private contacts, would have more credibility with our Western public than the superficial version generally meted out for Western consumption. We were sweating with the effort of trying to get across something much deeper: the notion that an honest 'warts-and-all' view of the USSR would, paradoxically, be reassuring to the average Westerner; the notion that flexibility and openness can be sources of strength, not signs of weakness. Ironically, this 'glasnost' (openness) is now the theme of Gorbachev's 'perestroika'. We were also trying to get them to see how persecuting the Group for Trust only played into the hands of those who tried to instil fears of Russia in our own society, how it really pulled the carpet out from underneath our own efforts to change public opinion.

The Committee, though still huffing and puffing about our undesirable associations with 'persons of no consequence whose only design was to wreck the State', agreed to co-operate with our proposals for a visit. But the next morning, Karman returned white-faced from a trip up to our hotel bedroom to say that there were two large men sitting, like sphinxes, on chairs too small for them either side of the door. She had had to pass between their blank faces to enter the room. This was incredible, but the next forty-eight hours were only superficially funny. Men muttering into radios behind their lapels, men in cars behind us, a huge, white whale of a man who jammed himself into the phone booth beside us when we tried to make a call . . . It was all so ludicrously stereotyped, as if Hollywood were shooting a location film about the KGB all around us. Yesterday, we were Peace Champions; today, apparently, we were Enemies of the State, to be treated accordingly.

What was really very frightening was that we did not know how far the anger of those we had apparently so insulted, would go. We knew nothing. Evidently someone had picked up a phone, orders had been given, and now well-dressed, hard-faced men lurked behind trees with cameras, followed us in cars, even gave us familiar little waves. One thing was painfully, and awkwardly, clear: the swift reaction pointed inescapably to a close connection between the Committee we had met the day before, and 'the organs' whose attentions we enjoyed right up to our last moments at the airport, when they surrounded us, grim-faced, to search through every scrap of paper in our bags. 'Here,' I thrust a bit of paper into the man's hand, 'have a peace poster – put it up in the Lubyanka – brighten the place up a bit!' But it was all very well for us to joke – we were getting on a plane. Our friends from the Group for Trust who had come to say goodbye, had to live with this.

But at that time a crisis seemed to have been averted for the Group. That summer they experienced a brief respite from intimidation. They held regular meetings and began to establish more links with the peace movements of the Western countries through visitors.

Karman and I spent the rest of the summer frantically organising the 'Big Visit', blithely oblivious to possible 'complications'. We recruited Russian-speakers to act as interpreters, we collected up thirty women, we all raised an enormous amount of fare money, we made complicated bookings and we communicated with the Soviet Peace Committee.

Three days before we were due to leave, our visit was cancelled by the Soviet authorities. 'Technical difficulties' they said, and wouldn't elaborate. We all met up anyway, and in the months that followed tried to hang onto our original aim. To negotiate the rock, we turned into rivulets: some travelled the following year as tourists, some with other 'peace delegations' that hadn't blotted their copy-books.

But retribution continued. In December 1983 Olga Medvedkov was arrested on the absurd charge of assaulting two policemen. By now, however, enough people in the West had heard of the Group and were convinced of their authenticity to voice a significant protest. It made a difference and the three-year prison-camp sentence doled out to Olga was suspended. That winter, as Olga's trial was repeatedly postponed and the protests grew from all over the world, it seemed as if more than just the fate of the Group for Trust hung in the balance.

I haven't seen Olga since that hot May week in 1983. When Jean and I applied to visit with eight other women, the two of us were refused visas. Karman was allowed in with the rest of the group but she was treated differently. She was singled out for bullying attentions by the well-dressed, sinister brigade; she heard herself described as an 'anti-Soviet element', and even when she visited Red Square the nearest Russians would melt away at the sight of her unpleasant-looking 'companions'.

However, Karman still managed to renew friendships begun on her previous visit, while her seven companions pursued a twenty-four-hour visiting schedule. In Leningrad, there was no sign of surveillance, the park seemed full of Lennon look-alikes, and there were disputes as to whether the 'Sasha' who is the subject of Caroline Westgate's story, was really a beautiful poet with an open house to all, or whether his apparent kindness was all part of a clever tactic to divert an awkward group of Western women. Or was he a simple black marketeer? The Sasha enigma seemed to embody the Russian enigma, and the arguments go on to this day.

The stories those eight women brought back with them became the foundation for this book. Some of them were delightful, some horrifying. When Karman went with two other women to call on a Moscow surgeon who was a Group for Trust member, whom we had met the year before, they found him outside his flat returning with bags full of food. 'They rang to tell me to go out today,' he said, 'I knew that meant I'd be getting some interesting visiters so I went out to buy some food for you.' This was the kind of cheek that made Volodya Brodsky no favourite with the KGB.

Inside the flat which he shares with his bed-ridden mother, the phone rings and he hands it to one of the women who understands Russian for her to listen. Someone on the other end is making threats. 'Get those women out of here at once, or the consequences for you will be grave, get those filthy (Russian swear-words) anti-Soviet elements out of your flat, we've warned you before.' She turns white, covers the mouth-piece, and relays what she is hearing to the others. Nobody moves. The surgeon puts the phone down. Then the bell rings. The women control an impulse to leap into the wardrobe. He goes to answer the door. Joke! There's nobody there . . . Later, as they walk away from the flat, a car swerves into them, causing them to jump out of the way. The men inside leer and grin. They say goodbye to their friend at the Metro, then turn for a last look, as a huge man rushes past them. Their friend has suddenly been surrounded. Karman runs back up the long ramp, screaming 'Leave him alone, you bastards!' and her companions run after her trying to prevent her doing anything stupid. When they look again, he's gone.

Later that year Brodsky was arrested and sent to prison camp for 'hooliganism'. His crime had been to give out leaflets in the street suggesting that the Soviet authorities should give more publicity to the 'Nuclear Winter' study. In 1986, in response to pressure from Western peace and human rights groups, he was released and expelled from the country.

I cannot describe such things without being aware that they confirm Western stereotypes about the USSR. But, the problem is, we had our noses rubbed in such stereotypes. These brushes with intimidation, slight as they were, leave deep and indelible marks, and it is hard to know what to do with such experience when one is trying to create goodwill. What kind of message, I wonder, did the Soviet authorities expect us to relay to our Western public? Were we supposed to glide tactfully over incidents such as I have described?

With hindsight I have come to realise that such questions, assuming a grasp of such a thing as 'public opinion', are pointless. There is no guiding, knowledgeable intelligence behind Soviet repression. They are the reflex acts of the State-licensed bully.

Meanwhile, 'Greenham Heroines' still featured on the Moscow newsreels. A year later, some 'Greenham women' were paraded proudly around Moscow's Eastern Bloc Olympics (and on our own News at Ten) while others, who extracted a Group for Trust member from a Moscow Police station, were given the 'beefy bloke' treatment (and were not shown on our news). It would be fascinating to compare the KGB and MI5 files on some of us.

Whatever the result of our efforts, it had certainly taught us a lot. Looking back on our story, I see us muddling across a minefield. We had asked for Soviet official co-operation in an exercise which invited people to behave as if the Iron Curtain were an unnecessary anachronism. This was plainly naive, or at the very least, extremely premature. We went to seek a reassuring message. We did not find the one we sought. The Soviet State does not want to relinquish its control of information, and hence its monopoly of contact between its own citizens and those outside. Yet we discovered that while the Group for Trust may be the only people to call openly for the barriers to be lifted, many people in the Soviet Union do feel that the Iron Curtain is an anachronism, and some young people are beginning to behave as if it is.

We also found that Soviet Society has many positive qualities which are evident in everyday life. What a relief to stroll around city streets and parks, for instance, free from that fear of violence that imprisons so many women and old people in the

West. What a relief to note the lack of garish, competitive advertising, and the simple, minimal packaging. What a relief to know that whilst 'full employment' often means menial, dirty or pointless jobs done by women for very low pay, at least the basic necessities of housing and heating are cheap. What a surprise to discover forests and beaches free of litter. In fact, one of the outrageous things we said at that meeting with the Peace Committee reflected a genuine admiration for some of what we had discovered. 'Take away the KGB,' we said, 'and in fifty years time you could have a country and a society that would be the envy of the world, one people would want to emigrate *to*, not out of.'

'Take away the KGB' . . . what a ridiculously naive thing to have said. But it raises a profound question, deeply relevant to our time. Can Socialism work without a repressive State which fears individual initiative and resists new ideas? And conversely, can one have the 'freedom' of Capitalism without the licence that ensures the rich become richer at the expense of the poor – and of the planet? What are the proper limits to each, and how can we find a new, non-military balance between the systems?

Our experiences did not cause us to despair, just because we found 'bridge-building' harder than we had anticipated. We glimpsed a little of what it is like to be non-conformist in a totalitarian society. Such a glimpse showed us that totalitarianism doesn't work and, in the case of the USSR, isn't working. It seemed to me that the 'threat' was not the USSR itself, but a society governed by fear, operating through mass conformity. This can arise in any society, and the Group for Trust were showing the only way, ultimately, to resist it – with human courage and spirit. Their vision – that ordinary people do matter and that, together, against all the odds, we can find the way to wrench the world away from its collision course with destruction – has been our inspiration.

This first story grew into a collection of stories by those who ventured into the poorly charted territory between East and West; they became this book, which will in turn, I hope, produce fresh stories.

Caroline Westgate
Official and Unofficial Peacemakers

Caroline Westgate is a potter who lives in Northumberland. She became involved in the peace movement because, she told me once, 'I couldn't stop the loop tape that went round in my head, whatever I was doing, of my children burning to death in a nuclear war.'

Peace activists seem to be flying by the plane load to the USSR nowadays. I imagine I'm in good company as I try to sum up my own efforts with the olive branch. Dealing with the Peace Committee, of course, felt qualitatively different from talking with 'ordinary' Russians. Their pronouncements were heavy with the sense of their 'speaking-on-behalf-of-something-bigger'. In that respect it felt exactly like talking to people with responsibility in this country. What was particularly Russian about those meetings was the sense that the members of the Committees saw themselves as the executive tip of a pyramid, not, as we might think of them, as powerful individuals operating in an authoritarian system. If they had power, or privileges like foreign travel, they would see that power as being justified and given dignity by the massive ground-base of citizens who willed them to their position.

The tremendous sacrifice made by Russians in the war, with

20 million dead and huge areas of the country totally destroyed, has left Soviet people with a correspondingly tremendous longing for peace and security. They use the word 'peace' like we use the word 'freedom'. It's a buzz-word, a synthesis of everything the nation stands for. Russians' desire for peace is evident everywhere. It's there in class-room activities, in Young Pioneer ceremonies, in huge street hoardings, in colossal street demonstrations, museums, war cemetries, and in war memorials with fresh flowers laid at them, often by wedding parties leaving the bride's bouquet. The 'Peace' slogan is so ubiquitous that some young Russians will roll their eyes back at the mention of it. 'Oh, *that*,' said 26-year-old Maria, with the air of one who has had it rammed down her throat since childhood.

The embodiment, as it were, of this huge collective longing for peace, is the Peace Committee, hosting hoards of foreign delegations, and explaining that the missiles of the Soviet Union are strictly for peace. Meanwhile, in another part of the planet, Western leaders are saying much the same thing. The Peace Committee man draws a distinction between *his* version of Peace through strength and the West's, by pointing to the different national and historical background from which his pronouncements come. Any uncomfortable parallels drawn between the East's and the West's contributions to Cold War hostilities are not the personal concern of the Peace Committee man. He is, after all, nothing in himself. He is but a small cog in a huge machine. He is a state employee. Not only is he powerless himself, he is relieved of the responsibility to change. Working within long-accepted parameters, pushing round his bit of machinery, he is an ordinary person, doing ordinary things.

The Medvedkovs, members of the Group for Trust, are the antithesis of this. Although they have no Party rank,* no position and no authority, they have nevertheless seized the responsibility for their own future. As we talked to them across their kitchen table we felt their strength, their sense of personal

*Yuri Medvedkov had been a Party member, but was expelled when he became a 'refusenik'. An internationally recognised geographer, he used to represent the USSR at the UN WHO – A.P., Editor.

empowerment. That is not at all the same thing as saying we felt
their power – far from it. They have no power at all, indeed
they have made themselves very vulnerable to the authorities
and have suffered and may suffer again at their hands. But they,
and the small but growing Group for Trust, are taking literally
the Peace Committee's oft-repeated slogan: 'Peace, the respon-
sibilty of each and every one of us.' One day, in May 1984, a
few of the Group went out into the streets of Moscow and
invited people to sign a petition calling for the resumption of
summit talks between the Superpowers. Nikolai Khramov, a
young student expelled from Moscow University because of his
membership of the Group, was wearing round his neck a Peace
Committee poster bearing that slogan. He and the others were
arrested that day, and the poster confiscated. As if that weren't
ironic enough, a few days later the Peace Committee sanctioned
a similar demonstration – and used the self-same placard.

What follows is a description of two meetings, the first with
the Peace Committee, the second with the Medvedkovs, and
the very different feelings they inspired.

*   *   *

The Peace Committee's offices are in a modern building on
Prospekt Mira. We are greeted in the hall by a good-looking
bloke in his thirties, who speaks impeccable English. The man's
name is Sergei Stepanov. He takes us to a small office where
there are armchairs round a low coffee-table. We introduce
ourselves and each gives a brief profile. Soon, Gregori Lokshin
arrives, an older man, and obviously senior in this outfit as he's
been to Britain many times and Sergei never has. Lokshin says
he can only stay for half an hour. We say good, let's get started
straight away.

He starts off with a long statement, outlining the Peace
Committee's work and explaining how it's wrong for us to think
of them as an official group, a branch of the Communist Party
as it were. They are funded entirely by voluntary contributions
and they exist because it is the wish of the people that they do
so. We have a list of questions prepared, so get down to it.

First, do they intend to show 'The Day After' on Russian TV? They have already shown part of it, says Lokshin, but not the whole thing because the opening scenes show the war starting as a result of Soviet aggression. This could never be. I missed the opportunity to ask why the Soviet people could not judge for themselves that this was a typical Western distortion. I'd also have liked to discuss the paternalism that Lokshin's answer implies.

Question two is: how much discussion is being given to the concept of the Nuclear Winter? Lokshin says everyone knows about it. Soviet scientists contributed data to research on the idea. There is a booklet published about it. 'What's the print run?' asks Fran. '200,000'. 'Well, you haven't printed enough, then,' says Fran, leaning forward and speaking quietly but firmly. Lokshin stiffens, evading the point.

We ask next about Civil Defence. We have noticed the curious slits in the Metro walls at the bottom of the escalators. Are these where doors will come across to close off the tunnels? Also, can they comment on a publication we've been told about, which advises Soviet citizens on how to shelter from a nuclear attack? We ask the questions politely. Lokshin is getting cross. 'There are no plans for the Civil Defence in the Soviet Union. Where have you got these ideas from?' 'People we have met told us it's what they believe.' 'In the Soviet Union, it is a crime to make propaganda for war,' says Lokshin, 'because this encourages war to happen. It's inconceivable that the Soviet Government would circulate such instructions. As for Metro air-raid shelter doors, perhaps that dates from an earlier time, maybe in the 1950s when there were fewer weapons and it was possible to think in terms of surviving a nuclear attack. This, of course, is no longer the case.'

We ask about the decree preventing Soviet citizens from having contact with Western visitors to the USSR. This suggestion is ridiculed. 'Millions of people visit the USSR; you have seen for yourselves the numbers of tourists around. Such a decree is a practical impossibility, unworkable.' (It passed into the Statute books in the following month, according to Western press reports). We say how moved we have been by our visits to

Soviet war memorials and say we fear that when VE day is commemorated next year the Russians' part in the victory over Fascism will not be properly acknowledged. We say we intend to campaign to see justice done in this respect. Fran mentions Jim Slater (Seamen's Union) who keeps on his desk the medal he was awarded by the Russians for his part in sailing three times to Leningrad to try to break the siege. We explain our plans for an exhibition of children's paintings and are offered some to take away now. We're very grateful for this.

Now the big one: 'Why is the Group for Trust being harassed?' Lokshin gets very cross. He asks why 'you people from the West keep on talking about this group?' He says they are 'refuseniks' or just people who want Western goods. 'And they will soon have their way' (i.e. they will soon be expelled). One by one we have a go at explaining why we feel the group has a valid idea and that they should be allowed to speak their views. We say that we agree with their perception of the need to build trust between individuals as a way of striking at the barriers that exist between East and West. I tell them about Sasha Bogdanov's remark, 'I don't know what the word border means. There are no borders.' 'Oh yes, there are borders,' says Lokshin, heavily.

We try to express what a distorted idea people in the West have of the Soviet Union. Because so few people come to see for themselves, it's easy for the media to manipulate the picture, by omission if not by direct lies. Fran says, 'Our propaganda is very subtle. We swallow the pill without noticing it! We also raise the point that it is extremely difficult for Peace campaigners in the West to answer critics who point out that we'd be locked up for demonstrating in opposition to Government policies in the USSR. When the Group for Trust is harassed it confirms Westerners' belief in the repressive nature of Soviet rule and reinforces their desire to defend their own perceived freedoms at all costs. People don't question the concept of the Soviet Union as 'enemy'. I quote the one bit of Russian I know, explaining that I learned it from a poster issued by the PC – 'Peace is the responsibility of each and every one of us.' 'Isn't that what the Group for Trust is doing,' I ask, 'taking

personal responsibility for peace?' I gather from the answer that
the obligation has to be exercised within a permitted framework
only.

We manage to keep it going even though the atmosphere is
very tense. As one of us finishes, sometimes close to tears,
someone else will take it up. Lokshin embarks on long
statements sometimes, gathering momentum like a steam roller
lumbering into action. In order to stop him from flattening the
dialogue, we occasionally interrupt. Gradually by keeping
going and keeping calm, the atmosphere improves and we
realise with surprise that Lokshin has been with us for one and a
quarter hours. About half way through we'd been joined by
Slava Luzhnivov who hadn't said very much. He leaves with
Lokshin. I say to Lokshin, 'People wishing me well on this visit
said "go and see the face of the enemy". I am pleased to have
met you, my friend.' He grunts and smiles.

We sit down again with Sergei Stepanov who is looking more
relaxed now his older colleagues have left. We talk for another
one and a half hours, going over the same ground we've already
covered, but in an atmosphere of discussion rather than debate.
Fran tells him of her experience at Geneva when, as a delegate
for Greenham at a disarmament conference, she had seen the
pointlessness of diplomats' elaborate manoeuvres, and vowed
never to try to emulate them. I feel the need to amplify why
Westerners have less trouble accommodating critics of official
attitudes. Once a government is elected, we are used to
no-holds-barred opposition being expressed. For us the right to
disagree with those in power is central and not unpatriotic in a
country where the Government is not the State. Significantly,
when we talk again about the Group for Trust, he says,
'Perhaps there is something in what they say.'

Afterwards he takes us to another room and shows us piles of
pictures and cut-out paper doves done by Russian children.
They arrive by every post, he says. One, a collage, is made from
bits of shrapnel from the last war. They are stuck on a bit of
card-board and form the letters HET BOЙHM! (No wars!) As
we leave, he doesn't shake hands, he grasps our fore-arms. He
looks at me very straight when he says goodbye and adds,

'Please believe I have a personal stake in this. I have a child who is one and a half years old.'

* * *

From the window of the Medvedkovs' kitchen there was a view of rows of modern blocks of flats, identical to the one we were sitting in. Dwarfed by these buildings was a little red brick church, its onion domes looking almost frivolously curly in contrast to the geometry of their surroundings. Yuri and Olga and their eight-year-old son Misha, had welcomed us with real warmth even though they had had several visits from Western peaceniks that day, and they had only moved into their flat that week. There were still packing cases in the living room, which was why we were sitting in the kitchen drinking tea and eating biscuits.

The conversation must have covered the same sort of ground as with their other visitors earlier in the day, but there was no trace of irritation in our hosts' replies to our questions about Olga's trial five months earlier. Their relief at its outcome was still very evident. Olga had been accused, on a trumped-up charge, of 'assaulting two militia-men'. Evidence at the trial proved that one of the officers in question was away ill on the day Olga was accused of attacking him. The verdict of the court had been 'guilty', but the sentence had been suspended. In the time between the charge being brought and the court hearing, tension had mounted. Olga had fully expected to receive a three-year sentence in a labour camp, and a KGB man had told Yuri that the baby Olga was expecting would be born in a camp 'and it would not be normal'. Olga described how she had said goodbye to Misha before leaving for the trial. He'd be 11 years old when she saw him next, she believed.

The Medvedkov's felt that pressure from Western peace movements had been a factor in securing Olga's release, and they were anxious to convey messages of thanks through us. But they did not want to dwell on the dramas of the trial. There were ideas to be exchanged, and future plans to discuss. Yuri explained how, since the Revolution, the Soviet Union has believed itself to be in constant danger of imminent attack. The experience of Hitler's advance deep into the country gave real substance to this, and the memory of suffering it caused is still very much alive. The Soviet army is a highly secretive organisation, and believes itself to be invincible. The Soviet Union's military power is not seen as a threat to peace, but a guarantee of it; the armies of the Soviet Union, by their strength, will not allow war. The Group for Trust recognises that to question any of those assumptions would be completely unacceptable, and they have been careful never to criticise the military policies of their country. They have based their campaign on the need for better knowledge of the Western world in the USSR, to try to remove the fear which has always characterised the Soviet's dealings with the West, working to replace that fear by attempting to build up mutual trust.

The Appeal with which the Group launched their activities was addressed to the Governments and peoples of the USSR and the USA. It stated that *'the balance of fear cannot be a reliable guarantee of security in the world. Only trust between nations can create a firm confidence in the future.'* The Appeal, a three-page document, was signed by the original members of the group, and hundreds of other people added their signatures to it. The wording was very carefully thought out, and nothing in it could have been construed as anti-Soviet. This was stressed by the Medvedkovs. 'If you see the Peace Committee,' said Yuri, 'ask them what it is we are saying that is considered anti-Soviet. Everything we do is open, and we are determined not to be driven underground as if we were doing something illegal.'

This openness has meant that the Group's members have attracted the attention of the KGB. Harassment has varied from the petty to the serious, and has been directed against relatives on occasions, as well as against the members themselves. Yuri spoke of the suffering and stress this has caused, but pointed out another result: the Group's decision to limit its contact with the world's press. Western newspapers are interested in stories of harassment, but won't print the Group's message. Press stories labelling them as 'dissidents' seem to justify the Soviet authorities' determination to marginalise them. They don't have to answer the arguments put forward by a group that can be dubbed anti-Soviet.

Sitting round a kitchen table drinking tea and eating biscuits made for easy, natural contact. It was easy, too, to laugh, to crack jokes, to relax into a warm conviviality, a feeling of having a lot in common. But as we walked away from the Medvedkovs' flat, away from the church towards the entrance to the Metro, brightly lit in the late evening gloom, we realised that we'd shared more than a sense of our common humanity. The Medvedkovs and the others in the Group for Trust are saying what so many in the Peace Movement in our country are saying: if you want Peace, prepare for Peace. The peace that is kept by murderous weapons of mass destruction is illusory and precarious. As the Group said in its original Appeal: '*Politicians on both sides are incapable of coming to an agreement . . . concerning any appreciable arms limitations, much less about substantive disarmament.*' They went on to say that: '*We all share equal responsibility before the future. Our common will for peace should not be blind. It should be expressed concretely, taking into account all the demands of the real situation.*'

While the Group appeals for more contact between the Superpowers at government level, they are also reminding ordinary citizens that they, too, have a responsibility to make peace for themselves. The climate of trust, the only one in which true peace will flourish, must be created at all levels. The idea that peace isn't something that will be achieved for us by politicians is central to the Group for Trust's thinking. Peace has to be built up, by individuals reaching across the barriers that divide East and West. Saying this, in the closed society of the USSR, is dangerous, but they *are* saying it and are prepared to take the consequences. The Medvedkovs and the other members of the Group aren't charismatic leaders or cult figures. But meeting them was very inspiring, because their determination to carry through their commitment to peace came across as a great inner force. It is not the first time in history that the politically weak and numerically insignificant have shown a true strength.

DIANA BARRATT

Militzia at Novodovichi Convent.

Barbara Doris
Frustration and Relief

Barbara Doris's dedication to war prevention began when she experienced the bombing of Liverpool during the Second World War. She took part in the first march to Greenham Common, was one of those who established the infant peace-camp and has been active in peace campaigns ever since.

Her first attempt to visit the USSR was thwarted. She was one of those 30 women whose trip was cancelled by the Soviets in September 1983. She joined instead a 'Mothers for Peace' delegation. Here she describes her own experience of meetings with the Peace Committee and, later, with the Medvedkovs of the Group for Trust.

At the end of our long flight from Uzbekistan, we were looking forward to refreshment and relaxation, but we were whipped straight off to see the Peace Committee. It was a horrific experience. Four of them and ten of us round a circular table. Uncomfortable earphones (not explained) for simultaneous translation. A camera whirring above the door. Sharp, side-stepping answers like those of politicians, to the questions we'd prepared so carefully. The translators were men, even when it was women speaking, and half way through one speech-like answer a translator with a Scottish accent changed to another with an American accent! It seemed to go on for ever.

When it was over we still didn't get back to the hotel for a wash, refreshment or rest. It was on to a prestigious Women's Committee meeting. When we got to their building, we had to face the TV cameras first; they wanted pictures of 'Greenham Women'. Our group wanted someone other than me to go forward, quite rightly, but I was being pushed. I stood my ground and then got angry and shouted, 'You refused visas to Greenham women. Now you're trying to find them in among "Mothers for Peace".' Yvonne gripped my shoulders gently and said, '*Do* you want to do that now, Barbara?' and I calmed down and managed to back away. Then we went into a hall with a huge table where about 100 women were seated. The speeches started up again; simultaneous translation came through slightly more comfortable earphones. I turned the sound off – I'd had enough. We still couldn't get away; we had to sit through a film before being released. When the meeting broke up, small groups of women came and chatted with one or two of us, which was the best bit of a tiring and largely pointless day.

Back at the hotel I moodily had dinner, unpacked and joined the others for a while when they were talking with Martin Walker, the *Guardian* columnist, before turning in. In the morning I remembered how Caroline had said, when she gave me the directions to get to Olga's, 'You may have to pretend you have the runs or something.' I didn't need to pretend! Eileen our nurse, gave me something to help it. The others were gathering to go to churches or shops, neither of which interested me. I wandered out of the hotel and then off to where I thought the Metro was. Was anyone following me? The Metro was not there and no one understood me – I was saying it the French way, I think. Then I saw people standing by a lamp post and taxis drawing up, so I joined them and was soon in a taxi asking for my destination. I still wasn't understood. I showed a paper with the address in English letters and off we went! Was anyone following me? I kept looking, but couldn't see anyone. We were soon there and I was charged five roubles!

I looked up the side road where I reckoned the entrance to Olga's flat was. There stood a soldier . . . I walked along the main road a bit, read the directions carefully, pocketed them and turned and walked back firmly. I was mentally practising 'Zdrastvuiche' to say as I walked by, but he had gone! So I climbed the staircase and pressed the bell, unzipping my jacket to show my Women for Life on Earth, Greenham Common T-shirt. The welcome was great. It was Yuri, Olga's husband, smiling warmly. What a relief. I was here and someone was in and I was welcome. So began a wonderful two hours.

I showed Yuri some of the photos I'd brought and he told me what they were up to – monitoring the media, worrying about Nikolai who was a pacifist (as they'd not broken the law before), having seminars. He told me about the harassment they'd suffered – one occasion reminded me of Karen Silkwood. He said that much of it was 'low-level' – not ordered but not prevented. That reminded me of Liverpool the night before the Corrie Bill, when some of the women arrested while protesting against this attempt to curb abortion were kept in the Bridewell overnight in disgusting conditions and taunted. He said they'd always written a formal complaint and had some apology (like some of our Merseyside Women for Peace when they complained about being strip-searched). He felt the Peace Committee was jealous of them; they could well be – he and Olga were so much better to listen to! They felt Olga would be given an amnesty soon, but didn't expect any more expulsions.

Olga came in when I'd been there a short while and Misha, their son, was with her, just come home from junior school. She made us some coffee and cakes and went to see baby Masha, two months old. I was then given her to hold. Later I went to see her cot, in the corner of a large sitting room, with Ann's mobile hanging over it. Misha was worrying about his homework. I could have been in a friend's flat in Liverpool. The kitchen–dining room was quite big and well fitted. Yuri had his typewriter and papers on the table.

I understand that foreigners are no longer harassed for calling on them; only young people are now. Eventually I had to tear myself away. I didn't want to go, but we were flying home that evening and there was a farewell meal in the afternoon. I hugged Olga. Yuri took me down in the lift. He was taking their

little dog for a walk and he directed me on my way back. I was
going to take the Metro but I'd cut it fine and I managed to get a
taxi back to the hotel.

*   *   *

On my return to the UK, as I relayed my trip to friends,
supporters and reporters, I tried to sort out how I felt. Of
course I want to go to the Soviet Union again and to encourage
others to go. I'm continuing to learn Russian, from classmates
as well as teachers and books, etc. I am more than ever sure
that the more we know and spread about the USSR, the more
folk will question the existence of the insane weapons we have
now. I am not sorry I went with a predominantly Quaker party
– they are trusted and I felt we got to meet folk that it would
have been difficult to find otherwise. But I don't think I could
face being part of a delegation again. I think it was the
assumption that we agreed with their government that bothered
me most and having to cope with an over-filled programme.

I keep saying I'd like to take a party of hill-walkers to
Kirghizia. I get to know folk better on the hills than anywhere
else; there I could begin the friendships I want to make.

Ann Pettitt
General Observations on Meeting the Peace Committee and the Group for Trust

We assume that, within the next few years, there will be many travellers whose impulse to visit the USSR, like ours, will be an outcome of their concern with peace-making. We don't want to discourage anybody from meeting with the Soviet Peace Committee and the other State organisations, such as the Women's Committee. But with the benefit of the collective experience we offer here, perhaps such meetings could be improved in quality and involve fewer set-piece repetitions of 'positions'.

When Westerners are prepared to ask awkward questions and say what they think, rather than feel they have to be polite and evasive, such an approach may be welcomed by some of the younger or more flexible-minded members of the party and state apparatus. The Western visitor is in a position to voice the things they may think, but can't (or daren't) say themselves. One consequence of the isolation of the Soviet population is that it is very difficult for Soviet bureaucrats to understand how others see them. We assume they know why Western populations fear Russia. But this may not be so.

The mutual lack of awareness between East and West can lead to all kinds of misunderstandings. A Soviet doctor who formed part of a Medical Campaign delegation commented that the English language booklet, 'The Soviet Peace Committee', states that: 'The Soviet Union has firmly pursued a policy of supporting national liberation struggles.' This, of course, implies that the Peace Fund could well be channelled into military support for the Ethiopean government against the Eritreans, and for the Afghan government against the Muhajudin. He also comments: 'There are, as we have learned, ample opportunities for visitors to the Soviet Union to deceive themselves as to what aims they may hold in common with the SPC, and this can lead to disillusionment.'*

I suppose our own story is a perfect example of such a misunderstanding, and it is not the only one. The Scandinavian peace women who first marched from Copenhagen to Paris, sought permission to walk through the USSR. The negotiations were protracted and exhausting, concerning how far they should walk and what the banners should say. In the end, they were allowed to walk a short distance through Leningrad and Moscow, where the Soviet public enthusiastically joined in by the thousand beneath a general: 'No to all nuclear weapons, East and West' banner. The original idea to walk the distance in between was somewhat modified.

A similar thing happened to a small peace group called 'A walk to Moscow', which set out from Washington in 1983, walked all the way across both West and Eastern Europe, but came to a dead halt at the Soviet frontier. Negotiations with the Peace Committee produced one excuse after another as to why the group could not walk along the road from Minsk to Moscow: they would not be able to buy food, they would get tired, there would be no hotels for them. The Westerners answered each objection, and finally produced a book of photographs recording a peace-march which had taken place in 1963, under Khrushchev, when a small group of Americans had walked the same route they were proposing. These people had, it was true, been accompanied by members of the Peace Committee, but they had held open meetings in villages along

*'The Soviet Peace Committee: Wolf in Sheep's Clothing?' by Stewart Britten, MRCPsych, in *Journal of Medical Assen. for Prevention of War*. No. 3.

the way, and held many discussions about peace and disarmament with the rural people. The Peace Committee representatives denied that the march had ever taken place, despite photographic and other documentary evidence. They finally admitted, after three days of stalling, that they had no intention of assisting the Westerners to achieve their aims and did not sympathise with such a method of 'struggling for peace' anyway. The Westerners left feeling that such an admission was quite an achievement: they drove in a bus from Minsk to Moscow.

These stories are an indication of the extent to which things have 'tightened up' since the Khrushchev 'Thaw' period. One common mistake underlying all these proposals for free-and-easy-contact to take place between Westerners and Soviets, *with the active participation of the Peace Committee*, is to assume that the Khrushchev era heralded a steady growth of liberalism, a relaxation of State control over citizens' personal lives, which has been proceeding to this day. There's no saying what developments between the State and the individual may take place under Gorbachev; the situation is no doubt very dynamic and could change quite fast; but at present it seems futile to expect, as we did, bodies like the Peace Committee actually to organise spontaneous grass roots contact, pen-pals, homely photo-swaps of families and the like. They're just not into it.

On the other hand, the Peace Committee, as many have pointed out, undoubtedly focuses a genuine desire for peace on the part of a public that really is sick and tired of war. Thousands of letters are sent to them on this theme, and also children's drawings and they're happy for Western visitors to take home armfuls of lovely paintings from Soviet schoolrooms which makes stimulating exhibition material back home.

It seems likely that small-scale meetings with Soviet organisations, involving few enough people for an escape from the 'question-answer' format, are going to have far more potential than large formal gatherings such as the one in which Barbara Doris found herself trapped. Many people are puzzled by the obvious contradiction presented by the Committee spokesman:* whilst claiming Western-style independence from 'the government' (which is not to be confused with the State) they nonetheless appear to be spokesmen *for* the State, and will never deviate from the current Party policy.

The clue lies in the nature of this one-party state. Since the Party alone has the 'correct idea', it is perfectly reasonable, seen from the Party point of view, that 'the Party' should play 'the leading role' in all organisations. The only way really to understand how the system works is to meet and talk with as many people as possible about the part played by the Party in their lives. The only way to understand how the Peace Fund is collected, is by the same direct method. The reality of people's lives in the USSR is not as simple as the view our own right-wing propaganda puts forward of oppressed masses maintained in subservience. However, the inevitable Party domination does produce a certain repetitiousness, to put it mildy.

If you do fix up a meeting with the Soviet Peace Committee, think carefully about what you want to say and what you want to learn. Try not to be fobbed off – you may have to put some questions several times before you either get an answer or a clear admission that you're not going to get an answer – and don't be afraid to interrupt if you find valuable time being taken up by long repetitive speeches.

You may want to ask questions about the treatment of people you have met whose peace initiatives are defined as 'hooliganism', but you certainly *do not* have to 'ask permission' from these committees to go and visit or to talk to other Soviet citizens. Nor should you feel any obligation to announce an intention to do so. You are not breaking Soviet law by making friends with people and you don't have to discuss your other relationships, although you may be asked to state your sources if it is obvious you have been talking with people. Regarding the answers you give, bear in mind that while the Committee itself is not the same thing as a department of the KGB it is, to

---

*They generally, but not invariably, *are* men, but a similar response will be had from the 'Women's Committee' which often hosts peace delegations, especially those organised by women.

put it delicately, part of the apparatus that includes the KGB. We must assume that information-gathering is part of the function of such committees which spend a lot of their time dealing with a section of the Western public in whom the Soviet State has a keen interest.

Sometimes photographs are taken (without asking permission first) showing visitors sitting cosily around the table with other Peace Committee hosts. These may then appear in the Soviet press, or in Peace Committee publications, as a way of implying a relationship between the Western peace movements and the SPC; the photos then appear in our own right-wing press as a way of discrediting the peace movement. This would have happened to us, had an undesirable 'element' – Olga Medvedkov – not been sitting there in our midst.

If you conduct correspondence with the SPC, allow plenty of time for letters. They do usually send replies to specific requests, but they don't engage in a discussion of issues by mail. Letters do reach them, but your replies may attract the attention of the British secret service, and they and other mail may arrive obviously tampered with. If this happens, take the matter up with your MP. You can write to the Committee in English and they will reply in English (if and when they do!) But it is difficult to arrange meetings at specific times from this country. If you make a trip to Moscow, you can telephone them or visit directly and ask to arrange a meeting.

*   *   *

The existence of the independent peace movement in the Soviet Union has always been extremely precarious. By attracting new members, the small group has managed to survive KGB intimidation, imprisonment of members in camps and psychiatric hospitals, and emigration and expulsions. By 1987 the Medvedkovs and almost all the original group members had been given exit visas (in the case of the 'refuseniks'*) or told to leave. Most are now in America. This mass expulsion happened

*'refusenik': a Russian Jew who has applied for permission to emigrate and been 'refused'.

DIANA BARRATT

after the Group protested publicly about the lack of information given to the Soviet and Western public after Chernobyl. In
the wake of the disaster, the group decided to oppose the
further development of nuclear power. Yet they remain
confident that the group will continue to evolve and survive
within the USSR. How it does so, and if it does so, remains to
be seen. Mr Gorbachev may proclaim a new policy of honesty
and 'openness'; but he appears as determined as his predeces-
sors to end the existence of independent peace initiatives within
his own country, even when those voices support his own
proposals, thus lending them greater credibility in the West. It
would be a sad thing if those openly offering hospitality to
Western visitors were forced to adopt furtive measures, in other
words to cease to function publicly.

But many times in the past four years I have been certain that
the group was about to fade out of existence, and each time it

has bounced back. Trust-building may have just reached the point where it can have a life of its own, taking protean form and myriad shapes, whatever the individual fate of group members.

Of course meeting the Group for Trust, in whatever form they continue to exist, is not the only way to meet and get to know Russians or the Soviet nationalities personally. Many of the encounters described in this book began in other ways. But their existence makes a small but crucial difference: anyone who visits can have at least one address of Russians who are prepared to offer hospitality to visiting Westerners. Furthermore, these people take upon themselves the responsibility for facing and coping with any unpleasant repercussions that may ensue from such contact with foreigners. That means that you do not bring them into greater danger by visiting them. On the contrary, by showing that you support what they stand for, you bring them not only a degree of protection but that solidarity which might just assist their survival as a grass-roots movement. Contrary to what the Soviet authorities appear to believe, it is not the CIA, but continuing support and visits from individuals in the Western peace movements which have helped keep the group going this far.

If you think you would like to visit the Group for Trust, you need to find out the latest situation. The addresses listed at the end of this section can supply you with up-to-date information and addresses in the USSR. Whatever the news, it will have been brought back by someone like yourself, so you should make sure you report back on your visit to a support group in this country, so that others can benefit from your experience and stay in touch with events.

Moscow addresses and up-to-date information on the Group for Trust can be obtained from the following addresses:

Peter Murphy, European Nuclear Disarmament, 14 Goodwin Street, London N4.

CND, 11 Goodwin Street, London N4.

Sergei Batovnin, P.O. Box 1073, New York, N.Y. 10034.

Trust Group Centre Abroad: Bob McGlynn, 528 5th Street, Brooklyn, N.Y. 11215.

Ann Pettitt and Linnie Baldwin
Meeting and Avoiding the KGB

This section was written with the assistance of 'Helsinki Watch', New York

We decided to include these comments on the KGB because so many people ask questions or would like to ask questions about the most feared and legendary aspect of Soviet life. 'Will I be followed if I try to meet people?' is the commonest question asked about visiting Russia.

Of course the editors of this book know next to nothing about the KGB: but, as it happens, we are in the relatively unusual position of having a little first-hand experience to offer. The question of how 'they' make their decisions, and what 'they' will or won't tolerate, is the subject of infinite speculation and beyond our scope – indeed, perhaps beyond anyone's scope. One day, maybe several life-times from now, historians will unearth the millions of files stored in the building on Dzerzhinsky Square (facing the department store 'Children's World'), whose interior is described in the final chapter of Solzhenitsyn's *First Circle*. Then maybe some light will be cast on events that never cease to perplex and amaze by their apparent absence of a rationale, but until then we must preface all our remarks on this topic with extreme caution. The KGB is a law unto itself.

Many visitors report after their trips to the USSR that they did not feel they were under surveillance or monitored in any way. Certainly the KGB cannot possibly keep tabs on every single traveller. But bear in mind that you are an amateur, and they are professionals. Although it may seem inconvenient and unnecessary, the simple precautions we suggest in this and other parts of this book are important if you want to make unofficial relationships and unscheduled meetings with people a feature of your visit. You will be helping both to ensure that a future visa application, if you make one, will be granted, and you will be saving your new friends from unwelcome attentions. The point about the secret police is that they are secret. When, as in the example we give below, they are obvious about themselves, that is deliberate and designed to intimidate.

The most important thing to say is that our experience was not typical for Westerners who visit the Group for Trust, or other groups of individuals who are in disfavour with the State. In our case, it seemed that they shrugged their shoulders at private meetings with the unofficial peace group, although outdoor gatherings with these people made them nervous enough to send several characters along to watch. What they really couldn't tolerate was our attempt to bring the sharply separate elements of Soviet society together in a dialogue: the Party-dominated committee and the self-initiated citizens' group. Or, to put it baldly, those who are in a position to give orders to the KGB and those who are its victims.

The following account by Linnie Baldwin of Karman Cutler's experience on her second visit to the USSR gives some idea of what Russians mean when they talk about 'harassment' by the KGB.

KARMAN MEETS THE KGB

Imagine you are in a crowded train, the Moscow Metro. Bodies tight against each other. You are tired. It is warm; sticky heat from the crush of people. You are going to visit a Soviet friend in the suburbs. Three English friends, separated from you by the crowd on the train, manage to find seats. You must stand. A huge man sits opposite your friends and merely stares. A prickle down your spine. Through the haze of warmth and weariness you become aware of another large man, very close to you, standing side on. His elbow nudges your stomach; once, twice with the rhythm of the train. His weight is a burden on you, and the elbow nudges once more and does not pull away. Rather, it begins to exert a steady pressure on the wall of your abdomen. The pressure increases to the point of severe discomfort, and then definite pain. The man turns to face you but the elbow does not desist. The large man's elbow is crushing you against the door of the train. You realise, suddenly, that soon, the train will stop at a station. You do not know on which side of the train the doors will open. The pressure of the large man's elbow is now extremely painful and enough to catapult you out of the train should the door to which you are welded open at the fast approaching station. Nobody on the train, except you and the large man himself, has any idea of the elbow's effect upon your stomach or on your frantic imagination. The elbow is perhaps about to cause a pointless 'accident'. What would you do?

She is very frightened but knows she must do something. Anger rescues her. She cannot scream. Instead she looks the large man in the face and whispers 'Get your fucking elbow out of my stomach,' with a vehemence that transcends any language difference. The man moves away. She walks across the train as it slows down, towards her friends. The huge man who has been staring at her companions jumps to his feet and places his considerable bulk between her and the others. One friend reaches over his shoulder and touches her – 'Don't worry, I'm here.' As they get off the train, the man dances between them, separating her. She feels walled off from her companions by large men. The strange ritual continues until, suddenly, the men just melt away up the escalator. As it happened she was not pushed from a train. As it happened . . . only the memory of her own fear of what *could* have happened and a livid bruise on her stomach remained.

*   *   *

This is the answer to people who say 'Oh come off it, it was all your imagination, how can you be so sure *that's* what was happening?' Until you experience something like this, it really is hard to believe. Our mild, Atlantic, British backgrounds do not equip us to cope with the fear this kind of encounter can engender. Karman is a woman dedicated to the removal of nuclear weapons aimed at Russians, and to the welfare of the unemployed of an obscure Welsh town. It seems particularly pathetic that such a person should be singled out for bullying like this. *Who*, one wonders, makes these crazy decisions. Who orders these time-consuming, pointless exercises?

For some reason we expect the KGB to be discreet about themselves, but they don't seem to mind being obvious: in fact, the intimidatory value of say, a couple of leather-jacketed guys literally breathing down your neck one minute, disappearing the next, and reappearing for no apparent reason later on in your day – is evidently the main point. In other words, they like to bully, and they like to keep everyone guessing, and wondering whether it really is true that 'they' can tune in to any phone in the whole country. They like you to think that they really are like 'Big Brother', and can know everything about everybody, and can do just what they like and get away with it.

So if you are being followed because your contacts are considered undesirable, or it is thought your behaviour might be embarrassing, you'll probably know about it and it will make you nervous, as it's meant to. Russians themselves, judging by accounts, vary wildly in their perceptions of how 'careful' they should be or what are sensible 'precautions' to conceal behaviour that might be construed as non-conformist – such as having Western friends. In a country where rumour replaces whistle-blowing, independent reporting, a little skulduggery goes a long way. Only one businessman has to 'fall' from his window to keep the Western community in Moscow on its toes, only a few Russians who've presumed to speak out of place have to meet with nasty 'accidents', to make everyone who feels those eyes upon them a little runny inside.

Although it appears that under Gorbachev the background fear generated by the presence of the KGB's network of informers is receding, you should still observe the following simple precautions if meeting people of any kind, unofficially or privately, is part of your programme.

Don't discuss your contacts in your hotel room or in the hotel restaurant, or with any people apart from those you know and trust. Use the hotel phone if you want to call official committees, but *not* private citizens. The taxis outside the hotels, which cater exclusively to Westerners, are widely believed to be driven by men who will report anything 'interesting' they overhear. So, if you're going to see someone, use public transport or your legs to get away from the hotel vicinity before resorting to a taxi. Never leave your address book or notebook lying around in your hotel room or in any official building. (For example: during a visit to the Women's Committee, a group of women were invited to leave their bags in an empty room. Returning unannounced to collect something, one woman found a man going through the bags.) Always carry notes and addresses with you, preferably in a pocket.

Make sure that if you're late back to the hotel, or miss your last Metro and have to stay away overnight, your companions don't panic and start calling the Embassy, the police, foreign correspondents, the morgue, etc. This kind of over-reaction can only create headaches and unpleasant questioning, and get you noticed which is what you want to avoid. If you're going off on adventures work out with your fellow-travellers a system that will leave plenty of leeway to allow for the fact that it is very easy to get lost in Moscow, and you can't phone the hotel and leave a message for your friends – they just don't do that sort of thing.

The fear at the back of the minds of many Westerners – that by stepping outside of the tourist 'gulag', they may inadvertently find themselves within the KGB 'gulag', is not realistic. It is evident from the accounts of visitors, that the vast majority who do take time off to wander, converse as best they can and make friends, meet only the rumours and not the real thing.

Of course there must be occasions when the KGB wants to check up on a visitor's contacts without that person's knowledge. If you really want to reassure yourself you're on your own in the city, then you could try getting snarled up on the public transport system for a few hours and take a good look at the faces around you: is there anyone who's been up and down and back again on the bus with you?

Common sense dictates that some behaviour is likely to arouse suspicion – such as poking around anything faintly military-looking, especially with a camera. After all, the West does operate a network of real spies, and the Soviet population is encouraged to be vigilant, and indeed to regard Western strangers with suspicion. Obviously you'll stand out more if you're wearing the latest flashy Western clothes (which, in the tourist areas, make you a hot target for black-marketeers), but if you are noticed as a foreigner, you're just as likely to be instantly forgotten.

Just because foreigners are unexpected, that doesn't mean they're going to be unwelcome, although the Westerner needs to be aware of possible Soviet suspicions. If you appear, in conversation with strangers on park benches, in cafés and so on, to be 'pumping' them for criticisms of their country, such as 'But isn't it wrong your country's got all these weapons as well?', then it should come as no surprise if the views expressed appear utterly conformist to government policy. Likewise, a Westerner should be wary of any Soviet stranger who appears to be keen to solicit 'anti-Soviet' views. In the end, it does indeed boil down to a question of trust and your own instincts about people. It would be a shame to police yourself away from possible fascinating encounters because of paranoia about the KGB.

The Foreign Office recommend that all visitors to the USSR notify them beforehand, and fill out a piece of paper with their details on it. If it worries you that innocent wandering might be misconstrued as 'spying', then it might be reassuring to know that someone can initiate enquiries should anything suspicious happen to you. Karman Cutler, suspecting that she might be singled out for attention, as indeed she was, left a letter with her solicitor, to say that she was departing in a state of sound mental and physical health, and to investigate urgently should she fail to return on the expected date! Whether you call this sensible or paranoid, it made her feel better.

If while you are in the USSR you have reason to be seriously worried for your own safety, you should immediately contact your own consular services at the Embassy, or a correspondent from your country. Make a note of the address of the Embassy before you leave. If you are asked to take part in a 'chat', in other words to be interviewed informally, you can ask to have a person from the Embassy present.

Don't mistake the Red Army, or the 'Militia' – the uniformed police – for the KGB. Both these categories of uniformed men can be safely approached for directions, and so on. Mind you, so can plain-clothes KGB men, but they might not be so helpful.

As to whether 'they' really do have every hotel room bugged, as the rumour goes – one might as well err on the side of safety and presume it's true. But it's rather like those endless speculations on the part of left-wing activists here who are convinced their phones are constantly bugged. Information-gathering technology is one thing – intelligent use of it is quite another.

Maybe whoever makes policy inside 'the organs' would like to know what every foreigner was up to, who was meeting who, and what they were talking about. But it's obvious that, however much they might like to keep tabs, they simply can't – there's just too much of it going on. The more Russians and Westerners meet as friends, the less enviable becomes the task of anyone seeking to control such a process.*

It may in the end be some comfort to reflect that, while the KGB has a reputation for ruthless efficiency, our own, albeit very limited, experience of the practice of surveillance leaves an impression of clumsiness and muddle, hardly relieved by over-manning. In the end, the secret police the world over seem to be better at scoring 'own goals' than anything else.

*See also introduction to 'Brief Encounters, Friends and Lovers' for a more detailed discussion of the 'rules' governing contact with people.

Ann Pettitt
Delegation Russia

Many visitors to the USSR travel the 'delegation' way, meaning they go to engage in some sort of official business with Soviet organisations. Such delegations are often organised by people within the broad spectrum of socialist parties and groupings in the West, such as Trades Unions, Socialist or Labour councillors, and so on. But you don't have to be 'pro-Soviet' to organise or to join a delegation. At local or national government level many people have visited this way who are positively antagonistic to the Soviet system. And recently groups within the peace movement have started to organise 'delegation' visits in order to find out more about those we are encouraged to regard as our enemies.

Inevitably, if you are going as a delegation you are asking the state to show you the country, and it is hardly surprising that a somewhat flattering and very 'official' view results. You may put in requests beforehand to be taken to places tourists would not normally see, such as places of work, but the selection of which particular places you visit is up to the authorities. Governments or local authorities in the West are not going to go out of their way to expose evidence of fundamental problems to visitors from the Eastern bloc either.

People who travel delegation-wise seem to be given very full programmes, which may well include a lot of 'tourist' sight-seeing, as well as the visits to factories, schools and so on. Crammed into a hectic schedule will also be long meetings with the host organisation.

From the accounts which follow, the limitations of a 'delegation'-style visit, particularly when it comes to opportunities really to *meet*, as opposed to *see*, ordinary working people are obvious. But official co-operation can also provide opportunities for meetings, generally with those higher up the decision-making ladder, that would not otherwise be possible. The experience of John Launer, the doctor who went determined to find out something realistic about Soviet health care, shows that the 'delegatee' does not have to be content with a superficial view. Both sides obviously appreciated the greater depth of exchange that followed from a little persistence.

While a delegation may not be the best way to sample the real flavour of the society and limits to random meetings may be greater than those encountered by the simple tourist, because skipping large parts of the 'programme' may seem less excusable, it remains the only way that professionals can be sure of having meetings with their Soviet 'counterparts'. The need to have a greater exchange of ideas, based on a truthful acknowledgement of problems, is so great that there seems no reason why those who travel by this route – to discover and to share ideas – should accept poor quality meetings in the name of politeness. The new policy of openness ('glasnost'), reflected by a willingness in the Soviet press to admit to the existence of problems, may well make such professional dialogues a much more worthwhile experience.

Nor do people *have* to be constrained by their pre-arranged programme if they have come with the aim of 'meeting ordinary people' and they find this is not happening. Once Westerners exercise their initiative a little, they are often surprised by the response.

In 'East-West Reach' Janet Tyrrel manages a spur-of-the-moment deviation from the official programme, and one woman who has travelled as a group leader with several delegations writes:

Two of my trips were organised by East-West Reach. They had arranged visits to kindergartens, schools, old people's homes, factories, youth clubs, peace committees, women's committees. This was in addition to sightseeing and we also had our own contacts; people went off independently doing their own thing, like visiting women's magazines, sketching, taking photographs off the beaten track, visiting and having meals with friends, in their own homes, which our media says one can't do. Once our guides/interpretors realised that we were a group who were perfectly capable of getting themselves about, who wanted to meet ordinary people, etc., they couldn't have been more helpful in finding out unusual things; in their experience most tourists behave like zombies and consequently go around in herds. Once they realised that we were passionately interested and anxious to learn, vistas opened up. We had long discussions on education, abortion, divorce, problem children, care of the old, the penal system, religion – you name it, we talked about it.

Questions of payments are decided between you and your 'host organisation'. To arrange a delegation, you need someone to make a preliminary visit to the Soviet host organisation, to explain what kind of programme you'd like. If you travel this way, don't forget you will be presented with gifts everywhere and you need a suitable supply.

Claire Ryle and Jim Garrison, who arranged several delegations to the USSR under the name 'East–West Reach', have produced a book which should be useful to people who want to arrange special-interest trips with 'counterparts' recognised by the Soviet State. The book, published by Merlin Press in early 1986, is called *Citizens Diplomacy: Exploring Anglo–Soviet Relations*, and is a directory of people who have experience of different fields of contact within the USSR.

Jean McCollister

DIALOGUE OR DIATRIBES?
Report from a US–Soviet Forum

Jean McCollister graduated from the University of Washington, Seattle and then continued her studies as a Rhodes Scholar at Oxford University. She now lives on a farm in a small, neutral, European country.

The second time I went to the USSR I was a member of a delegation of 40 young 'influential citizens' from America. It was the summer of 1982 – in other words, two years into Reagan's first term, and the question our Soviet hosts kept asking us was 'Have we reached the worst stage of our [US–Soviet] relations, or is the worst still to come?'. It wasn't just rhetorical. Really, what they were asking of us was to go home after the conference and talk some sense into the Reagan administration. Most exchanges between the US and the USSR had been cut off and this one, sponsored by a non-governmental organisation called 'The Forum for US–Soviet Dialogue', was one of the few channels of East–West communication still open.

The Forum was founded in 1972 and every year since then it has co-sponsored, with the Committee for Youth Organisations of the USSR (CYO), a week-long conference held alternately in the US and the USSR. The initiative was first taken at the dawning of détente but soon gathered a momentum of its own which kept it going even through the worst years of the second cold war. The idea is to recruit promising young professionals and students, throw them together with their Soviet counterparts, and hope that some East–West understanding and lasting relationships – smoothing the path for present and future US–Soviet co-operation – will emerge after two weeks of intensive talking, partying, and drinking.

That year the conference was held in the Siberian city of Irkutsk. The American group spent a few days in Moscow first, met by the usual welcome wagon of officials from various institutions of the Soviet establishment – the Supreme Soviet, the Central Council of Trade Unions, the US–Soviet Friendship Society, TASS and Novosti, etc., as well as sophisticated, intelligent researchers from the Institute for the Study of the USA and Canada, some of whom were included in the Soviet delegation. Once in Irkutsk we were joined by the rest of the Soviet delegates and broke up into 5 commissions which met daily for 3–4 hours at a time for the next week. This was where the real work of the conference took place. The small size of the group (10–15) and the intensity of the discussion encouraged a thorough exploration, both of contentious issues and of areas of prospective co-operation in US–Soviet relations, and was a welcome change from the superficialities, banalities, and outright lies frequently met with in larger, more formal gatherings.

My commission dealt with issues in science, technology and the environment. We were: myself, with recently acquired degrees in Russian and zoology and a strong interest in ecology and conservation; a lawyer with experience in environmental law; an agronomy graduate student preparing for a career in agribusiness; a computer scientist and a Russian-speaking, fisheries biologist who'd worked on Soviet fishing ships in the North Pacific and had had a hellish time getting a visa to the USSR, as a seemingly arbitrary victim of a recent, American-bashing campaign in the Soviet press. On the Soviet side: an honest, easygoing biologist from Novosibirsk; a bright and friendly economics student; an official representative of the

Central Council of Trade Unions who had already addressed our group in Moscow and alienated me with her hard line on the Polish Solidarity movement; a shy, earnest specialist in fish genetics from the Limnology Institute at nearby Lake Baikal; a cancer researcher from Latvia and a cocky but nonetheless likeable fellow from the US–Canada Institute with a practised American accent. As it happened, this same fellow was expelled from the US the following year when he foolishly blundered into an FBI trap whilst carrying out 'activities incompatible with his status' (a member of the Soviet mission to the UN) – seeking low-level, classified information.

In the course of the week we covered a range of topics, both concrete and abstract: space research, pollution, genetic engineering, abortion, whaling, and general questions about the proper role of technology in society. Although a separate commission had been set up to deal with topics in arms control and disarmament, this issue figured prominently in one form or another in all the commissions. It was inescapable – here we were, sitting round a table together (by mutual agreement Soviets and Americans were intermingled rather than adopting the usual conference table arrangement of Soviets on one side, Americans on the other), citizens of two countries hell-bent on stockpiling and aiming ever more lethal weapons at each other. One never forgot that. And so our group discussed the importance of avoiding an arms race in outer space, of developing joint projects in environmental and cancer research instead of weapons programmes, of using technology to better human lives, not destroy them. Nothing terribly original, but we were serious and we meant it, and came away convinced that the 'other side' meant it too.

On the whole the atmosphere in our commission was agreeable and congenial, unlike some of the others – Arms Control and US–Soviet Relations for example, where Soviet and American delegates rarely saw eye to eye on any issue raised. We were never allowed to forget, though, that the US was entirely at fault for the breakdown of relations between the two countries. It was the US who had cut off scientific and other exchanges, it was the US who had started and was now accelerating the arms race. Soviet policy was infallible and eternally peace-loving.

The persistent denial by the Soviet side of any responsibility whatsoever for the souring of détente was exasperating. The worst moments came during formal meetings of the entire delegation with long-winded Soviet official spokespersons. Since our group was meant to be representative of the whole US political spectrum, we had with us some Reagan supporters and analysts from conservative think tanks who could be counted on to react strongly whenever the Soviets tried to foist all the blame on the US. Question and answer sessions quickly degenerated into predictable 'what about . . .?' volleys: what about Afghanistan, what about Angola, Poland, Czechoslovakia, SS–20s, Sakharov, *ad infinitum*, provoking equally predictable 'what about . . .?' responses from the Soviets: Vietnam, poverty and discrimination, US support for brutal right-wing dictatorships, etc. Such exchanges were invariably reported in the final documents as 'an open and frank exchange of views', but really the whole affair was more like a Forum for US–Soviet Diatribes than a Forum for US–Soviet Dialogue. If East–West understanding was promoted at all by the Forum, it was only when this idiotic exercise of pinning blame and finding fault with the other side was abandoned, and people just talked as honestly and non-ideologically as they could about issues of mutual concern.

The problem with going as part of a delegation, of course, is the difficulty of meeting people outside the officially-arranged programme. Part of the problem is that you're made to feel so indebted to your hosts for their lavish hospitality, that opting out of the programme (especially, of course, if you do this in order to visit anti-social elements like refuseniks, human rights activists, or unofficial peace groups) seems like shockingly bad manners. Our delegation was given the full VIP treatment. We travelled in motorcades with police escorts wherever we went, and ordinary traffic was held up to let us pass, like Politbureau members on their way to a meeting in the Kremlin. Bands and ranks of Young Pioneers bearing flowers, balloons, and placards welcomed us at every arrival. We were wined and dined to the point of absurdity: once, on our way back to Leningrad from Irkutsk, we put down briefly in Omsk or Tomsk (I forget which and was so dazed by that time I couldn't have told the difference anyway) for refuelling. It was perhaps a forty-minute stop, and we'd already eaten on the plane, but immediately on landing we were ushered to a grand hall and a sumptuous banquet laid on by the local Komsomol – champagne, wine, vodka, caviar, platters of 'zakuski', the works. After a week of this sort of treatment I was feeling in need of a rest and took a walk in the fresh air instead. This was noticed by one of the Soviet organisers who let me know how I'd hurt his feelings by my rejection.

The other thing is that we were given such a full programme and kept so busy that one simply didn't have time to go wandering about making random contacts. Our Soviet hosts tried to satisfy our appetite for a taste of 'ordinary people' by farming us out to hand-picked 'ordinary families' for dinner one night in Irkutsk and staging meetings with 'the youth of Leningrad' at a sort of nightclub at the Palace of Culture. I asked the Leningrad youth I ended up sitting next to, how often he and his friends used the club. Never, he replied; he'd come tonight because the Komsomol had ordered him to. Real 'ordinary people' were in fact afraid to come anywhere near us, fully understanding that we were an élite group, privileged guests of the CYO, and gate-crashers would not be welcomed.

One afternoon during an excursion to an outdoor museum of Siberian architecture on the banks of the Angara River, I was bravely approached by a young woman when our chaperons weren't looking. She wanted to welcome the Americans but hadn't been included in the official welcoming party of singers and dancers in folk costume. So she decided to act on her own initiative. Pleased at finding an American with whom she could converse without an official interpreter present, she introduced herself, scribbled a few words of greeting into a slim book of poetry (her own), and gave it to me. She slipped away when I rejoined the group, but I saw her again briefly from the window as our buses were pulling out, taking us to the next stop – a youth sports camp. She was standing back near a row of trees, waving goodbye.

Although I was conscious of the actual and psychological crowd barriers which set our delegation apart from the population of the country we were visiting, I didn't necessarily feel constrained or deprived of 'real' dialogue by them at the time. For one thing, I'd already spent four months in the country as a student in 1979 and had had ample opportunity then to see everyday life in the Soviet Union and make friends with Russians, spending many hours chatting informally around kitchen tables. That had been one experience, and this was another. They complemented each other. I had been warned and criticised by friends and family back home in America about my proposed visit with the Forum; some referred to it contemptuously as a 'peace junket' and assured me that the Soviets I would meet would only be hacks, liars, and lackeys, the whole affair being just a grand propaganda exercise to dupe naive westerners. In fact I was extremely impressed with the intelligence, integrity, and genuine friendliness and concern of the Soviet delegates, a few obvious creeps excepted. So I was quite happy to concentrate on building up relationships on both a personal and professional level with these people to whom the state, in effect, had seen fit to introduce me, and looked forward to continuing them through correspondence and future visits.

But here I was in for a bit of a shock. One of the persons I'd become closest to shushed me in an urgent whisper when I made the mistake of asking for his address inside the hotel as we were packing up to go at the end of the conference. It would be better, he explained later in the open air, not to write to him as this would attract the attention of state security. I could phone him from Moscow if I ever came to visit again.

I felt hurt and bitter, not at him personally, but at the system which made it a potentially criminal act for people to become friendly with foreigners. What was the point of all this dialoguing, I thought, if it couldn't be sustained without always looking over your shoulder to see who was listening? Other little disappointments followed. One of the scientists and I had agreed, after the subject of genetic engineering had come up one day in the discussions, to exchange US and Soviet guidelines and safety standards governing biotechnology research. It was just an obvious and simple gesture, putting into practice what we'd all unanimously agreed was A Good Thing, i.e. East–West exchange of scientific information. I sent her a copy of the National Institute of Health guidelines soon after my return to the States, but I never got anything back. Maybe she never got my letter.

Some months later a new bit of Soviet legislation prohibited the release of any information from one's place of work without official authorisation, so if my friend *had* sent me something at that point I suppose technically she would have been breaking the law. This was the same scientist who'd been so indignant because the US had cancelled most US–Soviet scientific exchanges. I had come away from the conference thinking that individuals could pick up what governments had cast down, but later on I began to doubt and wonder how much citizens could do when the government kept their hands tied.

I had run into the basic contradiction of the Forum programme: it was 'dedicated to expanding people-to-people contacts between the US and the Soviet Union', but the Soviet organisation it dealt with was an arm of the CPSU* and was equally dedicated to ensuring that these contacts took place only under the control and in the interest of the Soviet state. It didn't automatically follow from this that these contacts, from the American point of view, were therefore worthless. In some ways they were very valuable, to both parties. But there was a limit to what they could accomplish, and I personally felt there was an element missing somewhere from the dialogue. I didn't come away disenchanted with the Forum, since on the whole I had found it a very positive and informative experience, but I did feel a strong urge to explore further opportunities for dialogue which the Forum, through no fault of its own, could not provide.

By way of epilogue: back in the West, I began to hear bits of news about the Group for Trust which had formed in June '82, about the same time I was preparing to go to Irkutsk. They
*Communist Party of the Soviet Union.

refrained totally in their public statements from assigning blame or responsibility to either side for the current problems in East–West relations, and just took up the question of how these problems might best be solved. It was their belief that mutual suspicion and mistrust were the root causes of the arms race, hence the name which reflected their goal: the Group to Establish Trust Between the US and the USSR. Various measures were proposed to put US–Soviet relations on a co-operative rather than confrontational basis, such as joint scientific and medical projects, better communication links between the two countries, more people-to-people contact, etc. Essentially, they were trying to initiate a détente from below as well as from above, an East–West dialogue that included private citizens as well as government leaders and organisations.

I was intrigued. The same spirit that took me to Irkutsk seeking dialogue and understanding, led me to Moscow at the next opportunity, to the homes of the members of the Moscow Group for Trust, because I believed it would be people like them who would be able to provide that missing and crucial element of the East–West dialogue. I still believe that.

DIANA BARRETT

Janet Tyrrel
East-West Reach

Janet Tyrrel, who pushed her youngest child 120 miles to Greenham Common in 1981, was part of the group of thirty women whose trip to the USSR was abruptly cancelled by the Soviets in September 1983. A year later she visited the USSR as part of an 'East–West Reach' delegation. These are extracts from her diary of that visit.

MOSCOW: September 10, 1984
The Hotel Cosmos was a huge, curved block of 26 floors, holding 3,000 people – another effort to reorientate, find the loos, the lifts, the restaurant. Moscow feels like a metropolis, new and Monday-morning busy, whereas Leningrad was more an over-grown provincial city, full of history.

After breakfast the hotels empty – fleets of Intourist buses take off with their different groups, each with a guide. You meet some of them again at the sightseeing, stopping-off places. Often, riding through the streets, watching people on the pavement, in the trolley buses, in their cars, you find yourself in parallel with another Intourist bus, *its* occupants looking out at you. It makes you very aware of being a tourist.

Irene, our Moscow guide, is smart, efficient and brisk and doesn't think much of our lazy time-keeping. We're taken to

Moscow University, on top of a wooded hill with a panoramic view of the river and the city; then to an ancient convent by the water where Peter the Great used to immerse inconvenient women. It's the little things I notice – in the middle of the lake there are two floating wooden things, like Noah's Arks, for the ducks and waterbirds. There are swans, dark-coloured pigeons, ducks and young fluffy sparrows. There is a sense of caring in the cities – more small playgrounds with little houses, wooden animals, slides and swings; parks and lots of trees. There doesn't seem to be pressure to fill every space with buildings.

Later a few of us went to try to contact a woman, a geographer, whom we had met when she was passing through Chester on an official visit. At her office they apologised and told us she was away on holiday. We weren't *quite* sure. In April when someone else had tried to see her, she had been on holiday then. But maybe . . .

We'd heard about long queues for shops, but the longest one we saw that day was for a temporary art exhibition. In the streets people stare at you and you begin to realise what they are looking at – sunglasses (few wear them), baggy trousers, and unusual shoes.

September 11
Another day that felt like a week long. First we visited a kindergarten with places for one hundred and fifty children from three to seven years old. It was orderly and clean but faintly shabby. Each age-group had a group of rooms – kitchen, play-teaching room, cloakroom, and rest-room full of ranks of little beds where the children sleep after lunch. Getting thirty three-year-olds to sleep at the same time made me wonder, but they denied any difficulties. The toys were adequate, though not plentiful – many coloured bricks, cheaply made large dolls, some books, basic equipment. Within the school there were two special groups with trained teachers for children with 'speech defects' which seemed to cover brain-damaged and subnormal children, those with cerebral palsy, etc. They were taught separately but otherwise integrated with the other children.

We were shown around inside while the children played

outside, then taken to a room where cakes, chocolate and fruit were laid out down two long tables. They had had very little time to prepare it and it was unexpected and extraordinary for the middle of the morning. Teachers and helpers came and had tea with us. We gave them gifts for the children, then went outside to see them. We blew up our peace balloons – they ran round with them, but didn't push to ask for them, nor complain if they had been missed out. Teachers and children had only returned the day before from their house in the country. We discovered that most schools and kindergartens have places for the summer (a form of holiday camp) which cater mainly for those children whose parents both work. We said goodbye to the head – a large woman in blue with fair hair piled up on top, wearing a badge someone had given her, saying 'Listen to Women for a Change'. The slogans of our women's movement had a certain inappropriateness, I felt.

Wednesday, September 12
Meeting with the Soviet Women's Committee in the morning. We sit round long tables in an imposing room. There are five women there – the Chairwoman (head of the information department); a sociologist; a doctor of medicine; a staff member in charge of contacts with the US, Canada and the UK; a staff member from the information department working with the press. We all explain who we are. It takes a long time.

Nelly puts her foot in it again, telling the Committee that people at home would dismiss our meetings as propaganda and not listen; that we need personal contacts, etc. I think it is a bit early in the meeting to bring up these delicate subjects. In any case the Chairwoman deflects the question and carries on talking about the structure of the committee, etc. I sit there thinking how extraordinary it is, three years on, almost to the day, to be sitting round a Table in Moscow, where Greenham seems to be a by-word. Remembering the difficulty of getting any coverage for the march from the press until women chained themselves to the railings.

We talked about currency problems and the difficulties of travelling. We talked about women, children, families. Barbara asked about work with alcoholics and difficult children. It's funny how, after a bit, all the information and its translation, begins to sound like gobbledygook. Sheila's eyes are closed; mine are closing; others looked glazed.

KIEV: Saturday, September 15

Secondary school visit in the morning. I had very mixed feelings which were difficult to sort out. We were received by the headmistress who told us something about the educational system and their school, sitting at a round table with some of the teachers and the older pupils around the edges of the room. Brown dresses, white aprons for the girls; brown suits for the boys. Red neckerchiefs for those in the Young Pioneers and various badges for members of various organisations. One young man was the head of those belonging to the Komsomol, the youth organisation of the Communist Party. Not difficult to sense latent hostility in him. He didn't look you straight in the eye and there was a sense that he was being polite very much against his will. I heard later that he had refused a peace badge, his reason being that he considered us linked with the American enemy.

I think it was the children who frightened me in some sort of way. They were very well-behaved – no hint of sniggering as I'm sure there would have been in some of our schools. The children all learned English from the first class and spoke it reasonably well. We had time to talk to some of them and I spoke to one or two of the girls. We were taken to see the Lenin room and various other projects which selected children talked about in turn (I had the impression it was well rehearsed). Then we went into the hall where the children were gathered – and it was disconcerting to be clapped as we went in. They sang peace songs to us and gave some recitations. What alarmed me most was the kind of aggressiveness with which they declaimed peace slogans. It seemed so inextricably tied up with the whole obsession with war, strength, militarism. The children were so unanimous, convinced, and single-minded in the presentation of an ideology, that for the first time I was uneasily aware of the complete conditioning of the children. A monumental woman in blue played the piano, turning the pages furiously. At the end she turned the book over and played without the music, a very vigorous tune. Everybody stood and sang. Was it perhaps the national anthem?

In the afternoon we visited Babi Yar – the mass grave of Jews murdered by the Nazis.

TBILISI, GEORGIA: Wednesday, September 19
Up early to write again. There is not much other time. I am lucky to have a room alone again. I like this view – the hill in front, squat below, river to the side and all the jigsaw roofs. It's not light yet but still there's a lot of traffic. The rain makes a clatter on the balcony. When they turn the fountain on, what a roar it makes. When the time is respectable I will ask the floor lady for a cup of tea.

Yesterday was another extraordinary day. Sightseeing tour in the morning – but since it was beginning with the funicular and some of us had already been on it, Sue, Nelly and I went off to get guidebooks for everyone, then got lost trying to find the end of the funicular to meet the others. We realised we were too far along, under the statue of Mother Russia on the hill. So we took a taxi to the old part of the town. We couldn't say much to the driver but made ourselves understood. He wouldn't let us pay and by gestures offered to take us round the town in his taxi. We refused as we wanted to go in and see Sioni Cathedral. There was a communion service in a small side chapel, with incense and singing. I presume it was an Orthodox service. There were bearded priests in long robes. You see few men with beards and I saw none with long hair. We walked across the river to the part of town with the oldest buildings and a small tower overlooking the river. You can tell it is a visiting spot by the number of parked Intourist buses. We found the others there, just leaving, so we decided to go on our own. We wandered through the narrow streets with poor-looking, dilapidated houses, many with vines hung with grapes.

A woman in red on a balcony asked us if we spoke English and warmly invited us in. Her name was Julietta. We talked in a mixture of very little English on her part, very little Russian (with the aid of the Penguin phrase book) on ours. Her flat was small – a tiny kitchen bit at the top of the outside wooden stairs, a living-room with a bedroom through a curtained alcove. She had a piano. Sue played *Für Elise*, then Julietta played and sang a Georgian folksong. She was so pleased to entertain us. She had a husband and a child, she said, and did not work. They were about to be rehoused in a new block of flats. We told her what we could about ourselves. We hadn't brought much that we could give but Nelly had a pack of felt tips for her child and I gave her the rest of my packet of cigarettes. She pointed to some religious pictures on her walls, said she was a Christian, and asked us if we liked them. When we nodded, she climbed on a chair, took down three from the few that were there and pressed us to take them. We simply couldn't. She had so little and they must have been precious to her. She didn't want us to refuse, but we insisted, not knowing really what we should have done. Sue took a photograph of us together on the steps outside and Julietta found us a taxi. Again the driver refused to take any money. There is a much more open feeling here than in the other cities and we are experiencing the hospitality for which the Georgians are known.

After lunch we went to the 'candy' factory. Marina, our Tbilisi guide, is small and well dressed with dark, sleek hair. I've caught her winking once or twice, showing a sense of humour our other guides have not had. The factory yard was full of ageing vehicles, lorries, and an old bus used for storing goods. A single railway line passed the yard to take the goods away. Some of the women were sitting outside in their white overalls and hats and more looked from the windows as we arrived. We all had to put on white gowns and were introduced to the woman director of the factory. Inside, we were taken very quickly around between the ancient machines, the sweating women workers, the conveyor belts of chocolates in various stages of making. Much seemed to be done by hand. We were offered sweets and chocolates to taste as we went round until we couldn't manage any more. An important-looking man appeared and stopped us taking photographs.

After our whizz round we were taken into the Director's

room where the now almost customary feast was laid out –
grapes and peaches, boxes and boxes of chocolates and sweets,
biscuits and cakes, champagne and cognac. Marina was with us,
Svetlana was with us too and a third guide had appeared from
somewhere. We asked the director questions about the factory,
and about women and work, showed our photographs, became
jolly with the champagne. Is this all routine for tourists? On the
one hand we are continually surprised by the hospitality we are
shown; on the other, uneasy about the lack of opportunity to
make real contact. We had little chance, for example, to talk to
the women workers. As we left, we were each presented with a
box of chocolates. Now I knew why so many guides came that
day.

Thursday, September 20
1.30 a.m. I can't sleep. My legs are aching and it's stuffy and
hot. The wooden bed creaks as I toss and turn. Suddenly I want
to go home. I'm tired of Mother Russia. But home is half of
Europe and two plane rides away.

   Later we went first to a tiny, very old monastery on a hill top
outside town, then down into the valley to the old capital of
Georgia to see an ancient cathedral. We walked a bit through
streets of old wooden houses, each laden with vines on trellises
or roofing the gardens beneath. The problem is that you are one
of many tourists in all these places. There are so many people,
you cannot take photographs of buildings free of them. We
complain of other tourists, being the same ourselves. But I
would prefer to do it differently. I feel conspicuous and out of
place. It's uncomfortable to be looking *at* people, impossible to
go unnoticed.

   After lunch in the hotel, back in the bus again to a place on a
hillside where they are making an 'architectural museum' –
moving typical old houses from different areas of Georgia and
setting them up on this 90-acre hillside site. Only some were
ready as it has taken time to move the houses and find authentic
furniture for them. But we saw two – one from each side of the
republic. The first was made entirely of wood, some of it
carved. It was a beautiful house of a well-to-do family with a

Chekhovian interior: woven rugs and bedcovers, a massive dining table, carved wardrobes, a baby's cradle. The kitchen building was apart, with a cooking fire in the middle, many utensils and garden implements, and worn, wide, comfortable wooden benches.

After supper Irakli from the Writers' Union came as he had promised, bringing the three of us books about Georgia and Georgian literature. He came with the other young man we had briefly spoken to the previous day. He wore the same puzzled, worried expression as he had when we first met him. He brought each of us a facsimile of the Georgian newspaper that carried the first short story of Maxim Gorky to be published. We promised to send them children's books, information about what is being published in the UK and said we would try to make contacts with organisations here. I gave Irakli the two novels I had brought to read as he was interested in contemporary writing. Now I have no fiction left. Rosalie and I can play chess on the plane.

LENINGRAD: Saturday, September 22

Home by tonight. A number of us have stomach pains this morning and decided it could have been the caviar last night. I didn't have the energy this morning to go the Hermitage or the War Memorial, both of which I missed last time. Last night and again this morning I wandered round the monastery grounds opposite. This morning there was a service on but people just went in and stood around. A bearded, legless monk pushed himself around on a low trolley. There were lighted candles before the icons, bearded and robed priests singing. We walked through the graveyards, the further one overgrown and derelict but very peaceful. Some graves with crosses, some with military decorations, many with fading photographs.

We arrived at Gatwick the same time we left Leningrad, 3.30 p.m. It felt extraordinary to be back after everything that had happened. Trying to get across London without an Intourist bus proved almost as tiring as my exhausting days of discovering Russia!

John Launer
Personal View

Before we set off we made it clear to the Russians that we
wanted contact with ordinary people, especially doctors. More
than anything, we wanted to exchange information about
everyday child and maternity care. Some of the group,
including myself, were members of the Medical Campaign
Against Nuclear Weapons, but we also included husbands and
wives, a 3-year-old child, a journalist, a photographer, and five
theatrical people who had come to meet the controversial
director Lyubimov and do the groundwork for an English
production of *Crime and Punishment*. On the first day we found
ourselves slotted into the formidable Soviet tourist sausage
machine; some of us absconded and saw sights of our own. We
contacted people whose addresses we had; I went to the races.
We also convened as a group and insisted to our guide that we
see what we had come for – hospitals, clinics, and kindergartens.

It was perfectly possible to do what you wanted. No one
followed us or even seemed to care. Individuals managed to
visit dissident Jewish doctors, successful academics, resident
foreigners, priests, and long-lost cousins. In addition, the
Russians were delighted to lay on 'special interest' events.

One visit stands out. In Leningrad we went to the Kalinin

District Maternity hospital, set among the dreary high-rise blocks that make up mile upon mile of the Russian urban landscape. Foreigners had not been there before. In the baby unit tightly swaddled babies, each with a number, were lying in rows and crying. Sixteen of them were being packed, four by four, on a trolley ready to be taken downstairs for their scheduled four-hourly feed. We sat down with a group of Russian staff and, gingerly, we raised Western ideas about bonding and separation. To our surprise, they were enthusiastic when we described our modern practice of 'rooming in'. They knew of such ideas and said that there was a lot of debate in the Soviet Union about changing policies. They would like to change, but it would be difficult because of the design of the buildings. Husbands, we learnt, were excluded not just from the labour ward but from the entire hospital. We exchanged opinions on supplementary feeds, induction rates, perinatal mortality, well-woman clinics, the respiratory distress syndrome, and neonatal jaundice. We were surprised at the rejection of the contraceptive pill as having too great a risk of side effects. The coil and abortion on demand are the Russian way.

Predictably, we saw some showpieces. We went to Moscow's Institute of Scientific Paediatrics, where Academician Study-entnik filled us in on official state policy and a digest of statistics – 115,000 paediatricians; 14,000 paediatric polyclinics; 180,000 beds; 15 million kindergarten places; special postgraduate training lasting six years; professors who must have 10 years experience and have trained five successful doctoral candidates. We also saw the exemplary special-care baby unit. Professor Galina Jatsyk took us through a discussion of phototherapy and necrotising enterocolitis and pneumothoraces.

In the same institute we visited a 'department of normative physiology' and found it a troubling place. Here 25 unplanned babies, mainly belonging to Third World medical students living in Moscow, are taken into care from birth to 18 months and used as subjects for intensive, non-invasive measurement and development assessment. The medical care on tap here is clearly the best that the Soviet Union can offer, and the atmosphere perhaps no bleaker than in some local authority homes, but it gave us an uncomfortable feeling.

The other showpiece was Moscow's Number 15 Paediatric Hospital, a converted ducal palace. As we stood in the glittering intensive care unit among familiar Western ventilators and dialysis equipment, Professor Minsdsa, paediatric traumatologist, held up x-ray films of severed limbs that his team had successfully regrafted to a child after a tractor accident. He also showed us the 'bubble' that they use for immunocompromised children.

Despite similarities, problems and differences were apparent. Professor Minsdsa told us that a major part of neonatal surgery is the correction of serious birth trauma. He also spoke of the 'excellent' ratio of one nurse to eight sick infants. Nursing is not a popular profession, whereas doctors are in ample supply. This hospital's complement of 600 nurses to 250 doctors is probably typical. One other striking difference in the intensive care unit, contrasting with the sophistication of the monitoring equipment and support systems, was the absence of parents. We noticed this in all the places we visited. Although mothers were allowed to breast feed on infant units, we saw none on any toddler wards or with older children.

We also gathered that hospital stays are long and made on less stringent grounds than is now fashionable in Britain. Children are sometimes kept in for several weeks or even months of convalescence while undergoing regimes of diet and physiotherapy. This may be followed by a stay in a sanatorium in the country. The uniformity of state education means that a child who moves from school to hospital to sanatorium will be following the same course of lessons.

The Moscow paediatric hospital had prepared for our visit, and a television camera was on hand. But some places were clearly not showpieces. We went to Yaroslavl, a provincial industrial city, and at one day's notice arranged to see a kindergarten for the children of workers in the local engineering works. It had its own full-time doctor, a staff ratio of one to four, and a large garden bristling with full-scale, coloured sculptures of animals. The children were neat and well behaved to a degree that made us almost nostalgic. They, like the buildings, had a 1950s air to them, and the community singing and paintings were in keeping with this. The facilities, however, made us envious. Kindergartens, like crèches and holiday camps, are provided universally, and even critics of the government speak highly of them. We asked in Yaroslavl if this excellent provision was a byproduct of the need for all women to work. 'Every mother,' we were reminded, 'gets six months' paid maternity leave, a further year's unpaid leave if she wants, and paid compassionate leave when her child is sick.'

We had, in the two weeks, dozens of discussions with individuals and groups. No one seemed threatened by contact with us or by hearing of what we do in the West. We did not find any subject, from Afghanistan to dissidents, that was unmentionable or caused any fear or embarrassment. One thing we did fail to see was a paediatric polyclinic. This was a pity because we would have liked to have seen how the complete division of adult from paediatric medicine works at the primary care level. In formal speeches our hosts often boasted of the multiple specialist services available in district polytechnics, as well as the domiciliary service and resuscitation ambulances based on them.

We went to Russia expecting a monolithic system of maternity and child care closed to investigation and criticism and suspicious of foreigners. We found the Russians to be surprised at our genuine interest and to be welcoming once our keenness was recognised. We found a familiar jumble of official facts and unofficial good humour and openness, and staff who like ourselves are hampered by history and economics but avid for improvement. The similarities were more striking than the differences.

Peggy Jones
Ten Days That Shook Me

TO SOVIET CENTRAL ASIA

I managed to pass the first fifty years of my life without the need for a passport. In 1984 I acquired one and used it twice, both times to visit the Soviet Union.

In May I was a member of the first group to travel with Dr Jim Garrison and Clair Ryle's organisation, East–West Reach, and spent two weeks in the USSR visiting Leningrad, Kiev and Moscow. Later, in October, I was fortunate enough to be offered a place on the Quaker organisation 'Mothers for Peace' delegation, which was hosted by the Soviet Women's Committee. The following are extracts from my diary written *en route*.

KIEV

One evening after dinner Joy and I left the Hotel Mir (Peace) in Kiev just to wander. One of my delights in a new place is to 'just wander'. We didn't intend to go far because we were both very tired. We passed a church, dingy flats into whose dreary entrances I peered inquisitively, a bookshop, and a fire station. There was a showcase outside the fire station with examples of how fires occur – frayed iron flex, broken glass and other things. We thought this was a good fire preventative measure. We saw a soldier sitting beneath a tree outside the door of the building.

We strolled on a little, then turned back. We both thought it would be a good idea to photograph the showcase, and Joy did so. Immediately the soldier leaped over to us, gesticulating wildly and speaking excitedly. He gestured us to a window, and called through urgently. I had a cold feeling in the pit of my stomach and Joy looked frightened – we had obviously broken some strict rule and were heading for dire trouble.

The soldier called to someone inside the building, received an answer, then motioned that we should return to the showcase. In great trepidation we did so. He pointed to the top frame of the showcase, where there were two red globes, then to the base, where there was a grey button.

He made us understand that when there was a fire he pressed the button, the globes flashed, and a bell rang. Now his face was wreathed with smiles. He wasn't a soldier at all, but a fireman, dressed in khaki with a red band round his cap.

How easy it is to have wrong assumptions.

TADZHIKISTAN

Sunday morning. A visit to a state farm; we were welcomed by the director in a large room, told about the produce and the lives and conditions of the workers (they had the most primitive lavatory I have ever seen!), then back to the coach to call on one of the workers and his family in his white, single-storey cottage.

We went down the side of the cottage into a shabby concrete yard – through an outhouse (was *this* the kitchen?) into a room with no furniture except a wooden cradle containing a black-eyed, dark-skinned, baby boy, a large television set, a tape recorder on the stone window sill and carpets on stone walls and floor.

A short, dark couple, he in shirt sleeves and she with a kerchief on her head and in a gaily coloured local dress with a small boy peering round her skirts. If they had known we were coming he would have shaved and she would have prepared refreshments.

She showed us into the front room, their sleeping room. More 'carpet' wall hangings, and floor carpet adorned with three sleeping mats. A large wardrobe against one wall, with cushions piled high next to it – they were used when sleeping in the iron bedstead in the yard in summer. She opened the door in the wardrobe, determined to find gifts for us. I saw shelves of beautiful, delicate Tadzhik china. She found bright, black-edged, silk squares – we were to choose one each.

Back in the yard – the kitchen and washroom were stone buildings at the back – admiring their orchard and animals. An old man joined us, he had been passing, saw us descend from the coach and wanted to know who we were and why we were there: he thought we were American. He made a long speech, and I thought I caught the word 'Churchill'. Translated from Tadzhiki to Russian to English, we learned he was 82, and had retired twenty-two years ago, had worked many years on the farm. Would we please go home and 'tell Mrs Thatcher we don't want war'. He wanted us to see his home and drink his tea but, alas, there was no time.

Back on the coach to our appointment at the home of a 'heroine' mother. Passing a row of semi-detached houses we were hailed by a woman – we must see her home. A long garden, turkeys, fruit trees, vegetables, outside loo (another hole in the ground), outhouse with cellar where grapes and other fruits were stored. Inside, there were three bedrooms. In fourteen-year-old, shy Grenadine's bedroom we admired her beautiful drawings. Downstairs in the sitting room there was a glass-fronted cabinet containing beautiful glass, china and silver and bearing family portraits, one of a son in the Navy. Sarah photographed three generations of women – old granny (who removed her bulky waistcoat to reveal a shiny green jacket), our hostess (a widow), and Grenadine. Grenadine and granny spread a white cloth on the table and soon a veritable feast appeared – wine, cheese, bread, pickles, sweets, strawberry preserves; eating, drinking, toasts to each other, to peace, to friendship, laughter, tears, warmth and joy. Our friend presents us with Grenadine's drawings; farewells and thanks.

On the coach again. We greet our 'heroine' mother waiting outside her home, her large sons hovering; a bed-table under the vines with sun dappling the cloth spread with another feast – if only we had known! Sitting on cushions, we eat more delicious bread and fruit, drink wine, smile, laugh, proffer small gifts and thanks.

One of our hostesses, Vera, a gentle, attractive woman, met us in the foyer next morning. After breakfast we set out for a meeting with the Soviet Women's Committee. Kzenia Prozkur-nikova was in the chair as the president, as Valentina Tereshkova* was in England at that time. Greetings were exchanged, we were given a programme and asked if we would like any alterations made. We were surprised and delighted to see that it had been arranged that five of us would spend four days in Kirghizia and the other five in Tadzhikistan.

I cannot do justice to the happenings of the next nine days. Next day we split into groups, one visiting a school, one a vocational training school and the third a women's polyclinic. I went with three others to School No. 21, to be greeted by the Director, the music teacher and the English teacher. First, the Director told us how the school was organised and the curriculum, then we were shown round by four seventeen-year-olds. The school ages ranged from seven to seventeen, and we started with the youngest. In each of the bright, cheerful classrooms we were greeted in English and entertained by jokes, short plays and poems, all in English, which became increasingly proficient as we went up the age range. The school has strong links with India, and we spent some time in the fascinating Indian Museum. Sarah, a fluent Russian speaker, recorded talks with children in most classes. It was difficult to tear ourselves away.

We all visited a textile factory, where the workers were mostly women. Not the Director, though! He told us the provisions for easing the lives of mothers at work – pay, conditions, holidays, nursery and kindergarten; we saw the

*The first woman astronaut, now rewarded by her position as President of the Soviet Women's Committee.

loom shop, first aid room, gynaecological room, dentist's room. One of our number was treated by the doctor for a very bad sore throat and another given a poster warning of the dangers of abortion after she had commented on it. We met women trade unionists, Komsomol members, women active in public life and both ordinary and specially proficient workers, and talked around a table laden with cakes and chocolates in a large room where samples of the materials used decorated the walls.

As well as the visit to the state farm in Tadzhikistan, we also met the deputy Mayor of the capital of the Asian republic, Dushanbe. We visited a hyrdo-electric power station, a kindergarten, were entertained by folk singing and dancing at a concert in a Trades Union Hall and had talks, wine and refreshment with the Tadzhik Society for Friendship and Cultural Relations with Foreign Countries. Everywhere we went we stayed over the time arranged. It was very difficult leaving for the airport, knowing we would probably never see most of these people again.

CAROLINE WESTGATE

PART TWO

BRIEF ENCOUNTERS, FRIENDS AND LOVERS

Introduction

Many people in the West don't think it is possible to meet Russians informally, let alone be invited home by them. Another popular assumption is that by meeting Russians and talking to them, you might bring them into danger with the KGB. The accounts of various meetings that we present in this chapter show that both of these ideas are myths; but like most myths, they also contain some elements of truth.

I've already mentioned in the earlier introduction the way that the system of unwritten codes of behaviour, known as the 'Iron Curtain', stimulates curiosity and interest in Westerners. But the eagerness of many ordinary Russians to meet and talk with Westerners is often blocked by this elaborate system of barriers. The tradition of 'pokazhuka' – distracting foreigners with a showy façade – has long been part of Russian culture and to a certain extent lives on in the receptions given to modern 'delegations' who find that 'visits' to places of work seem to be largely taken up by long meals with the management. This more formal 'delegation' experience has been touched on in Part One; here we concentrate on encounters of a more spontaneous nature.

It can be daunting to contemplate your special status as a foreigner: it appears to invest you with an unwonted glamour and gives you access to all kinds of consumptions denied the majority of the country's inhabitants. Sometimes you're not quite sure what lies behind friendliness: is it really interest in you, or is it because you represent the forbidden West? Is it your potential access to embassies and the Western press, those resorts for the desperate, the frightened and the dissident? Or is it just that you're a 'somebody' simply because you can skip in and out of shops and hotels and theatres effectively 'out-of-bounds' to all but a small handful of Russians?

Whatever may be the original motive, once you do start to meet Russians you tend to forget your original worries. David Baillie talks in his diary of 'all the things people find to talk about when they've been misinformed about each other all their lives'. It is this fascinating journey of mutual revelation around the gift-exchange of clothes or books for meals that makes even the briefest of contacts seem incredibly worthwhile.

This emotional charge is easier to understand if we bear in mind that the time when innocent friendship with a Westerner could be enough to ensure many years in an Arctic or a desert strict regime prison camp, is not so long ago. My own father, a member of the Communist Party in the nineteen-thirties, tried to visit a pen-friend while in the Soviet Union. To his horror he discovered he had 'mysteriously' disappeared. Experiences of such East-West friendship during what we now know to be the first climax of Stalin's terror, are a sobering reminder of the recent history which shapes the present-day response to the Westerner.

Things have certainly changed today, but the question remains to be answered: what are the risks, for Soviets and foreigners, in meeting? It is quite 'legal' to meet Soviet people. Recent decrees, however, nicknamed the 'anti-hospitality' laws, mean that it is now *illegal* to stay overnight at their homes, to get lifts in their cars or to collect substantial information about their work. Soviet citizens' perceptions of these new rules differ, however. No instances of attempted enforcement have been recorded. Some people seem to think these laws are effectively unenforceable; some officials, such as the Moscow Peace Committee, find them so embarrassingly archaic they flatly deny they exist.

It all goes to show that we cannot supply anyone with a crystal-clear list of rules and regulations, since we are dealing here with an unspoken tradition that is in a constant state of flux. From the State's point of view, the prohibitive effect of vague rumour is far more useful a barrier than a clear, verifiable, written code. Given this situation, it can be difficult for the visitor to determine exactly what is 'allowed' and what is 'safe'. The behaviour of Soviet people varies enormously, depending upon their experience, temperament, age and their feelings about the current political 'climate'. Some are keen to meet but are ultra-cautious, putting you into a taxi back to your hotel but urging you not to speak English in the taxi – just in case the driver suspects something. Others are relatively carefree and will happily be seen with foreigners in public places, even seeming to regard nonchalance about having foreign friends as a sign of sophistication.

Some may be willing to meet out of doors, but not willing to invite you home. Some may not mind coming to meet you at the hotel or walking you back there, others will want to avoid such places. Some will not mind being telephoned, others will. One thing to be borne in mind is that any person whose work has the remotest connection with military production will be forbidden by the rules governing their work from having contact with foreigners, and this may extend to their families as well. Huge areas of work are deemed 'military-related' although the connection may be extremely remote – the entire electronics industry, for example, falls into this category, and of course much office-work. There is a particular expression for this: it is called 'working in the box' because such enterprises, although very numerous, have box-numbers as part of their aura of 'secrecy', rather than addresses. But even here, one person's rule to be obeyed is another person's technicality to be discreetly evaded.

The best general rule we can offer is to show interest in people, but *let them decide whether and how to develop any relationship*. It is also not advisable to give detailed information on the phone (mentioning other people you are seeing, for example), and as a precaution against KGB interference avoid using the hotel telephones – walk a little way to the public booths outside. The KGB do survey hotels, with what degree of efficiency we shall never know, and 'bugging' of rooms is certainly not just a myth. If you follow these simple rules, you won't be beseiged by nagging doubts about possible repercussions to your contact once you're back home. It is considerate, too, to avoid ostentatious behaviour or dress when out with Russian friends or acquaintances, and generally to take your cue from them.

There's no point in denying that the Soviet State is still extremely nervous about the whole question of uncontrolled relationships between Russians and Westerners. Given this situation, it is inevitable that the Soviet people a Westerner meets will tend to have a more liberal-minded, risk-taking attitude towards 'rules'. However, in the present climate of renewed international tension, many conformist Russians may be keen to impress upon the Western visitor their own personal antipathy to war. If they are willing to talk, and there is enough common language to sustain such a discussion, they may well want to discuss further the aggressive postures of Western governments. Outright hostility has occasionally been encountered most commonly by Americans. (One American visitor found herself pretending at times to be Canadian.) But such hostility is the exception rather than the rule.

Emigration (often of Jewish families during the détente era of the seventies), though limited, has facilitated East-West contact. Often the first introduction into a Soviet household occurs because you happen to know, or to know of, a member of the family living in the West and you offer to act as a personal 'postman', carrying parcels, letters and messages. Once you meet one member of a family you may then go on to meet a whole circle of friends and acquaintances. More than one of the stories in this section illustrate relationships begun in this way, and the strength of Russian hospitality is such that a warm welcome will also be extended to members of your own 'circle' who may follow in your footsteps, bearing news, gifts, and so on from you – and so small but ever-widening networks are created.

A great many existing 'friendship circles' have begun in this way, sometimes as a result of relationships struck up by students who spend months in the USSR learning the language. It seems obvious to say it, but to meet people the best thing to do is to hang around where they do. This means wandering around places where people go for pleasure and are liable to be relaxed and unhurried. The parks in Soviet cities are wild, woody, lovely places, without the fearful undertones of violence you always sense in such places in the West; and walking and talking are well-established pastimes.

Some contributors have found that carrying something 'advertising' your identity as a Westerner, such as a Marks and Spencer carrier bag, or maybe a CND-sign carrier bag, means that Russians who want to get into conversation with you will approach you. Another suggestion is to keep an eye open for the small ads. which are stuck up on tree trunks, walls, sometimes special notice boards. If you can manage to read any of them, it may be that there will be some offering private English-language tuition (English is a very popular language). You could then ring up the number and offer some free English-language practise!

Another way to find contacts is through an Esperanto Club. This entails learning the international language, Esperanto, which is very popular in the USSR and Eastern bloc countries. It seems local Esperanto groups exist in most Soviet cities and will be able to provide informal hosting for visiting groups. Other 'special-interest' networks exist, such as that linking chess-players (John Roycroft's story 'Leningrad Wedges' describes a personal encounter with a Russian chess-player with whom he had corresponded.)

There seems to be no reason why more links on the basis of interest or profession should not be made – perhaps all it needs is for more people to take the initiative from this side. Of one thing we may be sure – and that is that such initiatives are more than likely to be received with enthusiasm on the other side. One senses that, whatever the politically conservative might think, the mass of Soviet people are more than ready to end the centuries of isolation which have so defined Russia's place in the world.

Unfortunately the context of a state leadership which is nervous about uncontrolled contacts of a personal nature remains. So, while trying to encourage people to get out and mingle, we also have to advise all sorts of cautions and devices which sound more appropriate to the world of pre-war spy stories than to the late nineteen-eighties.

The 'no-telephoning-from-the-hotel' rule has already been mentioned. This does not of course apply if it is an 'official' committee or person you're contacting. If you are lucky enough already to have some addresses of people to go and see, you won't want the customs man to find them (see Entering and Leaving on p. 198). It's hard to maintain friendships by post. You send letters, and don't receive replies. So you've no way of knowing if your letters got there. In the end, the only way is to make another trip yourself, or if you hear of a friend going over, give them a letter to deliver for you. Trying to give directions makes you realise how important it is to make proper notes of your visit. You need to remember not only the street, building number (korpus), floor and flat number but also the code needed to buzz open the entrance (podyezd). Note down as many extra 'markers' as you can (e.g. kiosks, playgrounds, other buildings). Memorise the route and write it down the minute you get back home.

It's difficult to know where to draw the line between elaborate 'precautions' which may in themselves lend an air of suspicion, and make a straightforward relationship seem furtive and guilty – and realistic consideration for one's Soviet friends. Soviet people known to be meeting foreigners may be interrogated about it by the KGB. This in itself is likely to involve no more than mild unpleasantness, but it is understandable, given the historical record of this State agency, if most people will go to some lengths to avoid such an experience. This makes the numbers of people who do offer hospitality to foreigners – and without any material incentive – all the more impressive. Our stories illustrate the difficulties, the fears and the rewards of such an experience.

D.I.Y. Détente in action:

The park bench

A 'stolovaya'

Official and unofficial traders

Official and unofficial youth

Group for Trust meeting in a Moscow flat

The Medvedkovs' kitchen

Red Army soldiers
with baby buggy …
and lollipop

TONE CONWAY

JOE CONWAY

Soviet women

TONE CONWAY

DAVID BAILLIE

Street scenes:
wild-mushroom seller

'Kvass' seller (refreshing drink made from fermented rye bread)

High-rise housing dwarfs old Orthodox church in Yugo-Zapadnya suburb.

DAVID BAILLIE

Harriet Franklin
Trying To Be Friends

Travelling to the USSR as a member of a peace delegation,
Harriet found this unscheduled experience was the most memori-
able.

I remember my attention had been drawn to him by one of our
group saying he looked like a priest. Half a dozen of us were
sitting out on the terrace of our Intourist hotel in Tbilisi,
mulling over the day's events and the merits of Gurjaani wine,
while we waited for dinner. The 'priest' was one of a party at
the next table evidently enjoying some kind of celebration. Our
two groups got into conversation and it seemed that one of our
neighbours was celebrating the arrival of a baby boy and had
brought his workmates out for a meal. Soon, photographs were
being passed round, toasts were being drunk and our corner of
the terrace took on the atmosphere of a party.

The 'priest's' name was Ilia and he was an economist. We
couldn't speak each other's language, so our conversation
consisted of sign language and drawings on scraps of paper.
When friends started to drift away we decided to continue our
'conversation' in the hotel's night bar. However, I left the bar
for a few minutes to find a dictionary and when I returned I
found that Ilia had been thrown out by the barman. He seemed

rather embarrassed by the incident and implied that Georgians were discouraged from mixing with foreigners.

We didn't want the evening to end on a sour note so we decided to try another Intourist hotel where, Ilia said, there would be dancing. We gave precise details to some friends about where we were going and left the hotel to find a taxi. I sensed things might be difficult when a couple of taxi drivers refused to transport us and the third only did so reluctantly. I assumed I looked unmistakably English and Ilia, with his aquiline nose and swarthy complexion, looked unmistakably Georgian! In any case, our trip proved fruitless. When we arrived at the other hotel I was told I was welcome to go in but Ilia was allowed no further than the hotel foyer. Sensing that our little excursion was attracting disapproval, I began to feel apprehensive. I had, stupidly, got into a situation where I didn't know the language, couldn't find my way back alone to my hotel and was dependent for my safety upon a stranger I couldn't converse with. I wanted to get back to my hotel as quickly as possible.

Ilia had other plans, even though he must have seen the look of fear on my face as the taxi took us on past my hotel and down the main street. (Still, perhaps he was more amused by the fact that our taxi-driver had now entered into the spirit of adventure!) We stopped outside a restaurant which only Georgians seemed to use and Ilia indicated that I was not to speak until we were past the doorman. The situation seemed farcical; we were acting like two criminals. Once inside, Ilia ordered food and champagne and we continued our stumbling conversation. He made me understand that he was also a little frightened but didn't mean to be intimidated by the authorities. He indicated that he thought it quite possible for someone to be listening to us on the other side of the wall. I wasn't sure whether to laugh or leave. I'd come to the Soviet Union to *explode* myths like these and I wanted it all to be a joke.

But I didn't leave because just then I heard voices singing softly in the close harmony that Georgian men are famous for and gradually others in the room joined in while the women sat and listened. The atmosphere changed; infected by the carefree mood, I began to enjoy the rest of the evening. Needless to say, when we left we used the same silly precautions going out as we had coming in, but, not daunted by our evening's experience, we decided to meet again the following evening, as it would be my last one in Tbilisi.

Ilia didn't arrive so I walked along Rustaveli Avenue for a last look at Tbilisi and returned to the hotel for an early night. At about 11 p.m. the telephone rang. It was Ilia. I went down to the foyer and found him there with two friends. They explained that they were late because they had been working and that Ilia had asked them to come along because one spoke German and the other English and he wanted them to act as interpreters.

Unwilling to be turned out of the night bar again, we decided to wander around the city. For an hour or more we walked and talked about life in Georgia. They had all been to university together and now worked in the same office. Then they wanted to know about English football, pop music, modern literature and all things Western. As we walked past Lenin's statue one of them spat in its direction and talked, angrily, about their frustrations at not being allowed to travel freely. They spoke of hating Moscow and of resenting Georgia's loss of independence. I began to think that, along with last night's singing, this was the 'real' Georgia – and far more interesting than meeting Peace Committees and factory managers.

Ilia lived close to the city centre and, in the early hours of the morning, we crept into his room. I could hardly believe what I saw. This was surely another part of Tbilisi the guides had forgotten to show us. Sparsely furnished, with only a bowl and jug for washing purposes, it all seemed so incongruous. But it seemed improper to ask what a university-educated economist was doing living in such a room, so we talked of other things. This was my last night in Georgia, so we all exchanged addresses and Ilia gave me his office telephone number in case I should visit Tbilisi again. Just before dawn, with promises of letters all round, we said goodbye outside the hotel.

Before we left for the airport, on a sudden impulse, I found my way back to Ilia's house with a farewell gift for his grandmother, whom he had mentioned but whom I hadn't met.

In the daylight the place looked even worse – peeling paint, rickety stairs, a courtyard full of noise and rubbish. Ilia must have told his family about his new English friend. They were surprised to see me on their doorstep and looked, with apprehension I thought, to see who else had noticed my arrival. But, once inside, they showered me with kisses and kind words and made me feel glad I had decided to make this last visit before leaving for home.

It's now six months since I saw them, but their warmth and friendliness, mixed with feelings of unease and tension that we were somehow doing 'wrong' in trying to be friends, have left a lasting impression. I am not surprised that I've received no letters from Ilia or his friends and I don't suppose they've received my letters either. Building bridges is a lot harder than I thought it would be.

CAROLINE WESTGATE

Ann Williams
Natasha and Olga

In June 1985, 46 women travelled by coach through the USSR to Odessa. The coach with drivers was hired from a company and the trip fixed up directly with Intourist. Ann Williams travelled with them.

When I first heard about the overland trip to Odessa with 46 other women I was tremendously excited. The reality proved to be even more exciting! Whilst still at the planning stage there was talk of possibly going to the Bolshoi Theatre, but unfortunately when we arrived in Moscow our guide informed us that it was impossible to get tickets. Many of us who had been really looking forward to this particular highspot of the holiday were very disappointed, and it was with reluctance that we accepted tickets to the Opera instead.

Despite all the wonder and culture of this great city, it is very short on places to drink coffee, and for an addict like me this is bad news. But I did in fact sniff one out, and found, to my satisfaction, that it had the reputation of serving the finest coffee in the whole of Moscow. It was here, in this rather grand hotel coffee bar, that I met Natasha. She was sitting at the bar, looking very distinguished and elegant. She expressed amusement at my feeble attempt to order coffee in Russian, and kindly came to my assistance. I was relieved to find she spoke excellent English and we quickly got into conversation. I found her easy to be with and we chatted about many things. I told her how we were not able to go to the ballet, and she immediately understood my disappointment.

I found that Natasha, like many other Russian people I met, had a great thirst for information about the West and a great desire to communicate with Western people. Perhaps it was the mutual knowledge that time between us was limited that caused the barriers to drop so rapidly. Natasha very soon was telling me her tragic story. In a low, grave voice she told me that her husband no longer lived with her. I sympathised, thinking she was divorced like myself, but I had misunderstood, her husband had defected to the West some years ago. She had had no communication from him since, and received no news of him either. She had some vague idea he may be somewhere in Philadelphia, but wasn't sure. I asked about children – she had none. She worked in a laboratory with chemicals that were so dangerous they had caused her sterility. It appears that her first husband (also a scientist) died as a direct result of working in the same laboratory.

It was interesting to note that during Natasha's intense and painful conversation, whenever the waitress came too near, she would immediately change expressions and become lighter as if we were talking of nothing more serious than the price of fish. She explained it was dangerous for anyone to talk to Westerners in this way, but she was prepared to take the risk because it was important for the West to understand how difficult it was for the Russian people. She spoke of freedom, and the difficulties facing Russian people who wanted to leave the Soviet Union. She lived in a flat where only a few weeks ago in the middle of the night one of her neighbours was taken away by the 'Authorities'. She had written some 60 or so pages towards a book she was producing. Natasha has not seen her since and doesn't expect to either. It appears Natasha's husband also took the opportunity to leave the Soviet Union in a hurry because of his 'writings'. She spoke fondly of books, and of her deep frustrations about not being free to purchase books of her choice. She said the bookshops that appeared to be overflowing with literature, were not what they seemed. The Soviet people could not simply go in and buy what the tourists saw – all the displays were for our benefit only.

After listening to Natasha's sad story, I wanted to do something positive for her. There was so little I felt able to do, but I did have a book which I knew she wouldn't be able to buy in Russia. So I arranged to meet her with the book the following day at the café. It was a book by a marvellous woman, Barbara Demming, a feminist and pacifist. I wouldn't have parted with it – except to Natasha. She warned me to be careful, that we could both be in serious trouble for such an action.

So at noon the next day, I found myself rather nervously drinking coffee and secretly placing the book, along with other goodies into Natasha's bag. It was over within seconds and the suspense was forgotten in the excitement of Natasha's next announcement. A ticket to the Bolshoi! She had queued for over four hours and managed to get me this highly prized gift. I had hardly time to catch my breath and take it all in, before I found myself being whisked over the wide, busy Moscow streets, dashed through the underpasses and pushed through the huge doors of the theatre itself. It was five minutes into the performance, and as I raced up and up this magnificent staircase I could hear strains of wonderful music. I was still shaking with excitement as I was escorted to a splendid gold-leafed box overlooking the stage.

The whole experience was overwhelming. Here was I, a miner's daughter, who had hardly gone further than Skegness as a kid, sitting in a grand, golden, almost royal box watching the ballet at the Bolshoi Theatre in Moscow – all on my own! During the interval I met my companions who shared the same box. They were Russian women. They were so kind to me, it didn't matter that we couldn't speak each other's language, we understood each other perfectly. They fed me with sweets and made me comfortable with their smiles. The showed me how to applaud and how to express disapproval, Russian style! They hugely enjoyed my enthusiasm for their dancers, and when I left they embraced me warmly, as did the two women who had taken care of my coat and shown me to my seat. I have never experienced such spontaneous friendship.

I was still trembling when I got outside to find Natasha waiting for me. She had waited throughout the whole performance. She knew our time together was at an end, tomorrow I would be leaving Moscow, and now I had to meet up with the rest of the group. We didn't say too much, other than promising to write, knowing the difficulties (Natasha's post was regularly tampered with) but choosing to ignore them. We hugged each other and smiled through our tears. We may never be able to meet again, but I will never forget her and she knew this. She had changed my life in such a short time, so deep was her message and her suffering. She stood watching me leave, this brave, lonely woman who shared with me her visions of freedom. I have written to her, but there has been no reply!

*   *   *

I found Odessa a comfortable place to be, the people were relaxed and happy, not least Olga and her family. I met her at our hotel – we were having a sort of farewell to Russia party and at the same time two wedding celebrations were going on. During all the gaiety my friend and I were invited to join Olga's table. This ultimately lead to us both being asked to spend the following day with them at their beach house. We were, of course, delighted to accept. Olga was studying English at night school and welcomed the opportunity of speaking her new language.

I must admit I was a little doubtful as to the genuineness of the invite, and wondered whether in the sobering light of a champagneless morning it would all be a big mistake. But not so. After a brief telephone call we were being taxied to an unknown destination, miles away from the safety of our familiar hotel. Both of us were feeling a little apprehensive, but all fears vanished when we saw Olga waving frantically to us as the taxi drew alongside her. She was so delighted to see us. She insisted on paying the taxi fare, and ignored our protests. She proudly marched us back to her small, three-roomed flat and introduced us to her mother-in-law and young four-year-old son. We were pleased to hand over some small gifts we had been able to collect from various women and, although quite small, they were received as if they were gold – it was like Christmas morning. It was quite obvious the family were poor, but so very proud, and generous. She gave us both books, and I have already spoken of their great value, and also a photograph of herself and son and husband so 'we would not forget them' – as if!

A friend arrived and after more introductions we were all trundling off on our next stage of the journey, carrying many bags of warm-smelling food. We eventually arrived at the beach house, which was in fact a small, two-room, corrugated hut. There were many of them in clusters scattered over the beach – a strange backdrop against the Black Sea. Nine of us huddled round a small table in the little hut and ate a feast which 'mamma' had prepared in our honour. We even had caviar which had cost them almost a week's wages! I really had to forget I was vegetarian, there was no way I could offend these beautiful people. Whilst being encouraged to eat heartily, we were bombarded with hundreds of questions about the West. They wanted to know about the fire at Bradford football stadium. Did we have lots of shops? Were shoes in London made of real leather? Did we like Margaret Thatcher? Do the unemployed young people sleep on the beaches? Is the miners' strike over?

Olga spoke about her concern and fears of the nuclear threat. Her wish was simple and clear that we 'could all live under the same blue skies and be as one people'; she was a mother troubled for her son's future. She would have loved to visit England, but she explained how difficult it was to leave her country. The authorities would take over a year building up a dossier on her, and it would have to be spotless, she would have to be in total support of the system and never have wavered or questioned it. She worked during the day in a warehouse as a 'worker' and her husband was a 'worker' on the railway. He loved English music, and I promised to send some tapes over for him of a particular group. He was thrilled to bits.

My day on the beach surrounded by all these people was wonderful. I felt so safe with them all, even though it was obvious from what was said that we were the only English people they had ever known to be on that particular beach before. In fact no one had ever seen any tourist of any nationality there before. I found everyone very friendly, with a warm sense of hospitality I had encountered many times before in this vast country. I was deeply moved by their genuine concern for humanity and their love of life.

Our farewells were again tearful, but tender and more hopeful about future contact. I have written several letters, but there has been no reply. I have sent the tapes as promised to Olga's husband – they were returned with the package slashed – the authorities had refused entry.

Caroline Westgate
Sasha

Caroline Westgate travelled with eight other women on a tourist trip to Leningrad.

I first saw him outside the hotel where he met us all, on Monday 18th June. Leonid was with him. Sasha was dressed all in white, with blue leather shoes, and looked very Western. There was a Swedish Christian CND logo on his sweatshirt. I was charmed by his gentle embraces when he greeted us. Leonid was more formal; he insisted, courteously, on carrying our bags. Enjoying the sun, the beautiful architecture, and the good company we walked along the embankment and over a bridge towards the Summer Palace gardens which we can see from our hotel window. It took us over an hour to do a twenty-minute walk. Sasha led us down the leafy avenues, between marble statues of figures from Greek mythology, until we came to a little round clearing in the trees where there is a statue of Krylov, the Russian writer who translated La Fontaine. Bas-reliefs of the animals in the fables are carved in the plinth. I had a quick go at sketching the scene, but it was more agreeable to chat. Everyone was very quiet, but very excited.

We walked on to the other side of the park, bought delicious ice-cream from a street trader. Sasha disappeared with Fran to buy bread and cakes. When they reappeared, there was someone else with them, another young man who was a colleague of Sasha's. Sasha explained that he only knew this man by sight, and had spoken to him for the first time in the bread shop, suggesting he came back with all of us for tea.

We crossed over a bridge, decorated with prancing horses, and doubled back again along the other side of the canal, to Sasha's flat. It had a yellow and white colonnaded façade and a faded elegance. There was dark green paint on the walls and graffiti saying AC/DC. Global Village.

The flat was big (especially for a single man in the USSR) and in a poor state of repair. There was some lethal looking wiring down the corner of the hall, the bath was in the kitchen, and the whole place hadn't been decorated for years. A vine house-plant had been trained round the kitchen walls, and a bunch of prickly twigs had been arranged in a wreath over the light.

In the smaller of the two living-rooms was a Japanese stereo system, and a lot of Western pop music on records. There was a day-bed with a rug over it, a heavy old table, a shiny wardrobe, a desk with a map of USSR above it, and a table lamp, with a shade made out of wrapping-paper. Sasha took me into the other room and explained how last night, when the other women were here without Joan and me, he had opened up his table so it was very long, and had laid out cakes and cups, flowers and candles, to make an impromptu meal.

He disappeared into the kitchen to make the tea. Back in the smaller room with the others, I put my Greenham wire, decorated with purple, green and white ribbons on his desk. He wants to make a collection of Greenham photographs to show his friends. I was delighted to have found somewhere so special to put 'my' bit of fence. Everyone was deep in conversation. I withdrew into a corner of the room to survey the scene. I felt very at home. It all seemed, as Ann Petitt once said, 'so ordinary and yet so special somehow'.

Suddenly I was overwhelmed and started to weep uncontrollably. It was the shattering realisation that this ordinary, familiar, everyday occasion, this meeting of friends, this strolling along home for tea, this easy, normal, human contact was agonisingly and simultaneously the exact opposite. The paradox was that nothing at all divided us, and yet everything did.

I sat on the floor behind an armchair, hoping no one would see my tears, but Leonid did. This quiet young man had been playing the supporting role to Sasha's central performance, mostly because he didn't speak much English. Instead of ignoring me he came across the room to offer comfort. Taking a tissue from my bag and wiping my eyes he said: 'Please, don't cry,' then, by way of explanation, 'It's a song, yes?' He may not have had much English, but he found the right words for me. All I managed to say, as I sat on the floor holding this young man's hands, was that I was weeping for everything that divided us, because there should be no divisions.

Sasha brought a trolley in, with tiny porcelain tea cups and a big plate of cakes. We had to eat quickly because it was time for the boat trip. Leonid escorted us to the canal, because a phone call had announced the arrival of Sasha's mother. Leonid took us back over the bridge to the landing stage. There was some sort of a mix-up with the tickets. 'Typical Soviet Union,' said Leonid. It seemed that the 8.15 boat, for which we had tickets, had gone, though it was only just 8.15 and there was no sign of it. The boat now boarding, we were told, was the 8.30 boat, and it was full. We wondered if there ever was an 8.15 boat. We argued a bit but gave up. We were about to go, but were called back. It seemed we could get on the next boat. Leonid saw us aboard and watched us from the bank as we chugged away. His face was grave and unsmiling. An hour ago I would never have thought it possible for such a man to reach out and comfort a woman inexplicably weeping.

I heard a lot about Sasha from the others during the week in Leningrad. There was a particularly baffling incident when he introduced his local Komsomol leader to the Western peace-women in his flat. I'd taken part in somewhat agonised discussions about the implications of that. Was he a KGB man engaged in some double game, luring people to his house to get information about their Soviet contacts, who could then be compromised? I was unable to form a rational judgment, being without any of my normal frames of reference. I could only trust my instinct.

On our last day in the city, Sunday 24th June, Joan and I set off to try to phone Sasha. Joan had sat up half the night writing on the backs of a huge pile of photographs which she wanted him to have. I was carrying *Christian Faith and Practice*, an anthology of Quaker writings. I marked a passage for Sasha which seemed to me to sum up what I was trying to do on this trip: 'A necessary condition of closer union is that we should get to know and understand one another better, and find out how much we have in common . . .' We tried a couple of times to get through to him from a phone-box , but there was no reply. Feeling very disappointed, we turned back to the hotel. On the bridge we came across Terry, a delightful old bloke in our tour group who was here on his summer holiday. Terry, who comes from Halifax, had had quite a few chats with us, and had evidently been doing his bit towards creating 'a necessary condition of closer union', by selling some of his clothes to black-marketeers. He explained that he was waiting for one of them now. Terry wanted to tell him he'd decided not to sell him his shoes after all. I was just thinking how glad I was that *my* contact with Russians had been on a higher plane when Terry said, 'Here he is now'. We turned round – and it was Sasha. He was still wearing his all-white gear, but I noticed that the white sweat-shirt was distinctly grubby. I felt quite resentful that Terry had shared Sasha too. I was selfishly glad that they finished their business quickly, and Joan and I took one of Sasha's arms each and steered him away from Terry, back over the bridge away from the hotel, and into the gardens of the Naval Academy.

We sat on a bench there, and Joan went through the pile of photographs. Sasha seemed delighted to have them. He scrutinised them intensely, and asked a lot of questions. He was puzzled by one of a block of modern flats in Newcastle which is being demolished. 'Why is this being done?' he asked. Joan explained that they had been built badly, they were beyond repair even though they were only about 20 years old. Sasha was astonished, as well he might be. He came to one photograph of a couple of young boys, Joan's god-children, sitting under their Christmas tree opening their parcels. They are both wide-eyed with excitement. Sasha studied it for a long time. 'I cannot believe these boys will ever hold guns in their hands,' he said at last.

I gave him my book, and some CND balloons which Hilary had said he'd asked for. He seemed pleased. We talked about our plans for Moscow, and told him we were wanting to see the Peace Committee. He shrugged. 'They're just bureaucrats doing a job,' he said, without malice. 'And the Women's Committee, they're the wives of Party men, and this is their charity work.' He seemed to dismiss both groups as an irrelevance. He had a look through my scrap-book, and was very interested in the photographs of our street theatre group performing in the Market Place in Hexham. I explained that the play is a short mime sequence which shows the symmetry of the arms race and how the sufferers in a nuclear war will be the Ordinary citizens, the dupes of the leaders of East and West. Sasha nods slowly. 'When you see the Peace Committee,' he said, 'ask them whether I, Sasha, could go out of my flat on to the street and do these things. Ask them that.'

Then he began to talk about his own plans. He said he wanted his house to be a place where people could come and find out about Western peace groups and what they were doing. That's why he was so pleased to have the photographs. He talked of the importance of building links with one another. 'What are borders?' he says. 'There are no borders. I don't understand what the word "border" means.'

It was time for us to go. Both Joan and I were in tears. We walked slowly, each hanging on to one of Sasha's arms again. I was frightened of the danger Sasha could get himself into. In his present way of life he was operating in the broad margin that seems to exist in Soviet society between what is legal and what is not, and he can do that in relative safety. But I feel, from our conversation on the park bench, that Sasha could see that beating the system wasn't going to be enough. He was going to have to try to change it.

Just before we reached the bridge, an extraordinary sight

made us stop in our tracks. The tarmac of the road was shifting. It was cracking and breaking up as we stared at it, and water was oozing up between the cracks. 'It's a water-pipe that's bust,' said Sasha. Just that – what a relief! For a moment I'd thought the ground was crumbling beneath my feet. Sasha said he would go and find someone to report it to. He told a story against himself, how once he'd called out the fire-brigade to a fire that had proved to be a janitor burning rubbish.

Laughing and crying at the same time, we kissed him goodbye.

DIANA BARRETT

David Baillie
From Russia with Love

Who says you can't hitch-hike in the Soviet Union? Here as always it proves an invaluable way of meeting people. This is one of several episodes we include in this section from David Baillie's diary of his extended visit. He shows how, with some preliminary preparation, he pre-arranged his itinerary with Intourist and the Soviet Embassy in London to include visits to places relating to his own professional interests, such as a power station. With a large dose of initiative and the gift of the gab, even a complete non-Russian-speaker can make personal and professional contacts in Russia and see beyond the superficial.

TASHKENT: 25th May

I've spent just a couple of days in Tashkent, but they turned out to be two of the most memorable of my entire visit. Owing to a typical Intourist mix-up, I found myself waiting at the airport for a non existent 'transfer' into town. In the end I hitched a lift in with a local man who said he was keen to practise his English. He invited me to spend the following day, a Sunday, with his family. It was a wonderful experience! Valentin, his wife Maria, their 7-year-old daughter Iya, their 17-year-old son and his girlfriend and their unofficial British guest, headed for the mountains 100 kilometres or so from Tashkent. We might have been heading to the Lakes from Wigan; there were stops for pop, to look at the view, to pick flowers, and to buy cherries. Then it was home to a magnificent family dinner in their typical Soviet flat. Traditional Uzbek dishes, fresh fruit, cherry wine, Russian champagne – and a feeling of friendship that transcended cold wars and iron curtains.

I was somewhat surprised to find that Valentin was Professor of Nuclear Physics at a large theoretical physics establishment. On his study desk at home lay an invitation to take part in a conference on particle physics in Chester. Five years ago he said he would have been able to go. Now, in the interests of world 'stability', he would be unlikely to receive the necessary permission to visit Britain. His particular field is purely theoretical with little or no implication for weapons technology, yet a field with a major role to play in our understanding of physical reality. Paranoia on both sides of the world now means that he and his counterparts in the West must waste time and resources following the same goal independently – even when that goal is understanding a common reality.

MOSCOW: 3rd June

Last day in Moscow today. I am sorry to leave and say goodbye to so many new friends like Olga and Ivor Polyanov. They are a father and daughter whose Baptist faith has brought them into conflict with the less generous side of Soviet Government. We started talking after they had approached me in Moscow's famous Gum department store. They were having a hard time trying to emigrate and had a constant KGB tail for their pains. As we walked around Moscow talking about all the things people do talk about when they've been misinformed about each other for decades, we were 'watched'. Every few streets one of these Le Carré figures would pass us on to another colleague who would stay with us until we left his particular patch. At several points we were photographed by a not particularly convincing looking tourist.

A few days ago I visited them in their Moscow flat. Olga is in her early twenties and speaks several European languages fluently. She had once been selected for the Bolshoi, but now

writes and sings her own religious poetry, and paints the most
remarkable icons I have ever seen. That afternoon we took the
train out to their country cottage or 'dacha' – even dissidents
seem to have second homes! We talked and gardened into the
evening, and I learnt about both the harassment by the Soviet
authorities, and the more subtle manipulation by governments
on *our* side of the Iron Curtain.

Their understandable disaffection with the Soviet system had
led them to listen to Western external services, especially
'Voice of America' and the CIA's very own 'Voice of
Freedom'. For six years these two disinformation services had
shaped their world view every night. The effect was as
disturbing as the harassment by the KGB. Both father and
daughter were convinced of a land of milk and capitalist honey
just the other side of the Iron Curtain; a land of great
peacemakers and humanitarian leaders like Reagan, Pinochet
and Zia; a world where nuns had to be shot in El Salvador
because they had been drugged into terrorism by the Nicara-
guans; a world where black South Africans have the vote; – a
world concocted out of the sinister imagination of the American
Right.

Between them, the governments of both East and West have
managed to terrify and brainwash this meek and peaceful pair. I
left them feeling anger that neither side in the Cold War felt
able to tell the truth about their own society to the other side,
nor to tell the truth about the other side to their own people. No
wonder we have wars.

Olga asked me to deliver a clandestine letter to the British
Embassy. I agreed, although I had an intuitive feeling that our
Government delights in exploiting the plight of Soviet dissidents. Their inaction over similarly persecuted individuals in
the West points only too clearly to their lack of moral integrity
in these matters. Reservations apart, it was an interesting
excursion. Outside the Embassy gate are the Soviet sentries
who check your British credentials. You then walk three metres
beyond the red stars and the kalashnikovs, and you are in
England – twee, pretentious, middle-class England. The wives
and daughters of the predictably male diplomats are playing

tennis in the garden; Ford Sierras are parked in the drive; and the air hangs heavy with public-school arrogance. My meeting with the Cultural Attaché was short and sweet. I handed over the letter, taking care not to give any oral titbits to the electronic eavesdroppers outside. The Attaché and I exchanged a few meaningless pleasantries, and I recrossed the Iron Curtain. It was a strange half-hour.

Yesterday, on my last full day in Moscow, I had arranged to visit Olga and her father once more in order to collect another letter. I took the train out to the 'dacha' with another English friend called Julie. Despite the careful planning the 'dacha' was deserted. Back at the hotel I received a call from Olga but the line went dead before she could explain what had happened. It was an uneasy way to say goodbye.

Another new friend I'll be sad to leave is Anna, a dancer with the Moscow Ballet. We'd met when I'd become hopelessly lost at an early stage of my apprenticeship on the Metro. She spoke about as much English as I spoke Russian but friendship seems to have its own international language and communication did not prove too problematic. We spent a typical Muscovite evening together – walking in the parks, watching children playing in the colourful playgrounds next to every housing block, and generally lazing around in a way the Soviet people are so good at. Dinner was delicious and included strawberries and cream, and potent red cherry wine.

I tended to carry my phrase book everywhere, but intimate occasions like this allow little scope for such indispensible phrases as, 'I think the carburettor is blocked' or 'Where can I hire some water skis?'. There is one section in the Berlitz Russian phrase book on 'dating'; the key opening lines, according to this authority on Soviet social etiquette are: 'Would you like a cigarette?' and 'You've dropped your handkerchief'. It doesn't leave much room for healthy non-smokers.

Anyway, in the interests of détente, it was after 9 the next morning when I returned to my hotel, much to the consternation of Intourist. Staying out at night is a crime punishable by a life sentence of excursions and transfers as far as Intourist is concerned. The secret is to take your hotel key with you on overnight visits. In this way Intourist finds it hard to prove your absence and it is possible to get away with just the unforgettable glowering of the ogres that Intourist place on every hotel landing.

*   *   *

It's certainly not easy to generalise, especially after such a short and limited visit. One impression does however remain fixed in my mind. This concerns the contradiction between a sophisticated, educated and relaxed younger population, and the severity and rigidity of both their elders and the State. The former are a product of the considerably increased standard of living associated with the Brezhnev years. This generation has not only come to expect far more in the way of a relaxed and materially well-off life style, but have become far more educated and aware of their situation than their parents and grandparents of the Khrushchev and Stalin eras.

But the State and its control are still in the hands of this older generation. Thus the Government and its immediately controlled agencies such as Intourist, Aeroflot and the Energy Ministry are still trapped in the grotesque inefficiency of a system originally developed for a society far removed from the aspirations of its people in the 1980s. Everything is so huge that response and reaction times are unacceptably and dangerously long. There is no doubt Soviet scientists, and indeed the Party themselves, are aware of the problem of acid rain for example, and do want to do something about it. But whatever the urgency, change can only occur at the desperately slow rate allowed by the cogs of this crazy system. It will therefore be at least five years before any actions is taken on acid rain – and maybe 25 years until the State finally admits that economic development is a function of efficiency, not size.

The growing gap between the Soviet people and the lumbering machinery of their government, seems to be one reason for the collective and institutional paranoia that results in such senseless harassment of dissidents, and the isolation of the whole nation from the rest of the world. I say paranoia because there seems little logical, political reason for such actions. The desire to emigrate by some Soviet citizens seems to be more in response to those aspects of the system that perpetuates this national imprisonment, than a rejection of Soviet society itself. It's such an illogical situation because, by and large, the Soviet system has so much to be proud of. The average provision of housing, education, child care, medical facilities, transport, etc., is far higher than in most Western countries (though the word 'average' is crucial). And yet Soviet citizens are denied the freedom to see for themselves the benefits of their own lifestyle in comparison with people on the other side of the Iron Curtain.

Hopefully, one day, the many Soviet friends I have made will have the freedom to visit England. Similarly, maybe one day in England we will have an equal freedom of access to medical, educational, and housing facilities now enjoyed by those same Soviet friends.

It's a crazy world, made even more crazy when you actually meet, talk with, smile with, and hold the 'enemy' whose indiscriminate slaughter our so-called defence policy is based upon. We have the capacity to kill 7-year-old Iya and each of her 270 million neighbours 50,000 times over, and they have the capacity to inflict the same insanity on us. Planning for her slaughter once over would be enough to justify the absurdity of 'deterence'.

I have a picture of Tashkent given to me by little Iya, with her name written proudly on the back. Even once would be once too many.

John Roycroft
Leningrad Wedges

John Roycroft runs a chess magazine which has Russian contributors. Here he visits a chess end-game expert in his home.

The bus rapidly rocks and rolls east across Alexander Nevsky Bridge, beyond my street and metro map. Right. Tallinn Prospect. Left. Krasnogvardeiskaya Street. Miles of it. There is nothing to see except ten-storey blocks littering the townscape like a nursery floor after a jelly party. After fifteen minutes Alyosha goldfish-mouths 'next'.

Sveta is expecting a baby in two to three weeks. She and Alyosha are very happy. They have their fourth-floor apartment, where they have lived for just a fortnight. It is communal of course, but the facilities are shared only with an amenable working lady. Into the flat, a couple of steps, turn right into the living room. The eye takes in the room in half a glance; the first thing to notice is the sloping window-ledge. Then the table, two chairs, sofa, book-case, TV. Miniature cacti make the window-ledge into a garden.

The hospitality is great, but not lavish. No alcohol, but diluted blackberry fruit juice. Alyosha and Sveta ask how I live. I ask how they live. Instead of being proud of my four-bedroomed, semi-detached, corner property and garden I am defensive and self-deprecating. There is a nearby wood (I had not noticed) where the mushrooms in the hot dish had been gathered. Did I go mushrooming? Not in London NW9.

The conversation is desultory, hampered perhaps by neither Alyosha nor Sveta knowing English. Sveta was orphaned and Alyosha had lost his father some years ago. It seems wrong to enquire more closely. They met at work. The photograph album shows the wedding, relatives, the supportive and friendly fellow-workers substituting for missing family. I tried to say the right things.

There is a bedroom, but I didn't see that; the baby would be in there. The kitchen adjoins the square living-room; the L-shaped passage leads to the door. Outside, the cramped lift and other doors. There's worse in Britain, but this is standard, for everyone. I would have nightmares about fires. 'Did they not have the right to larger accommodation?' I asked, forgetting they had just moved in. Apparently not, and what was wrong with what they had?

Alyosha, a near genius at composing chess end-game studies, shows me the pick of his latest achievements, and we forget Sveta for a while. She sits happily alongside. She'll return to work after six months. The black-and-white TV tells of British football hooliganism.

It was time to go. Alyosha and Sveta accompany me to the stop. I tell Sveta that there are at most four or five other chess composers of Alyosha's age and talent in the world. Alyosha hops around, pretending not to listen.

Once again on the 155 bus I remember what I have given Alyosha and Sveta. A puny, polythene baglet of marshmallows – 'konfety?' they ask politely – and a copy of the British Airways give-away monthly *High Life*, with its conspicuous consumption advertising aimed at the well-heeled passenger. What had I done? Forged a link, or driven a wedge?

Jaqui Marson
Ordinary People

'But how did you meet people – do you speak Russian?' I was constantly asked on my return from a two-week holiday in Moscow and Leningrad, bubbling over with stories of the people I'd met and the things they'd said. I don't speak more than three words of Russian, but more Soviets than you imagine have a fair smattering of English, or will rush off to find a friendly translator, so keen are they to converse. My friend and I met many warm and friendly Soviet people through peace movement contacts, but others became friendly after smiles exchanged on buses or park benches leading to arm-waving and international charades before an English speaker was produced. An evening spent with such people was guaranteed to produce a wealth of fascinating information.

I remember Masha who, like many a slightly bored young wife I know in England, encouraged intrigue and excitment. One night she had arranged for us to go and interview some underground rock musicians and was positively gleeful that plans had become 'a little difficult', It means we could have a little party instead.

Plans often seemed to become a 'little difficult' at the eleventh hour in the Soviet Union, especially where groups of people were doing things considered 'unofficial' by the author-

ities. But such difficulties were always met with inventiveness
and if you asked why, your naive question would usually be
answered with a shrug and a patient smile. 'It has become
impossible to meet these people, we will go and make a party,
no? People must not work all the time, you work too hard.'
Masha continued to put on her mascara, a present from some
Western visitors. This was going to be a Night Out.

The door bell of her fifth-floor flat rang; her friend Volodya
had arrived to pick us up. Volodya was a fascinating enigma. At
the tender age of 23 he had his own flat, his own car and an
incredibly stylish, Christian Dior jacket. No one in the Soviet
Union is homeless, but it is almost impossible for a young
person to get their own flat until they marry or start their own
family. He seemed to have acquired his through a complicated
series of deaths and divorces in the family. He lived where the
authorities believed his step-grandmother (now dead) still
resided. 'I am very lucky,' he said, modestly, though I think
cunning would have been a better description. 'My car, I won
her in a street lottery. I bought a five-kopek ticket and found
myself with a car.' Petrol, he explained, was very expensive and
difficult to find at the petrol stations, but he bought his from
lorry drivers who wound on their speedometres and sold the
excess on the black market. As with many things, and in
common with many people we met, he described this as being
'half illegal'. 'You see, you must understand our system. The
government know all these things continue but they understand
that without them we would all come to a halt. The black
economy is very important, but it is also important that you are
not caught.'

We stopped at a nearby Berioska shop in an Intourist Hotel.
This is probably the greatest way to endear yourself to your
newly made Soviet pals, who cannot get half the goods sold in
these special hard-currency shops, or, in the case of booze,
would have to queue for hours in their own shops.

Half of bottle of Barclaycard-bought vodka later, Masha and
I were sprawled on Volodya's bed discussing the universal
dilemmas of women while the men, Volodya and my friend,
were banished to the kitchen. The Soviet Union claims great

equality between the sexes, but what is it really like for women, I wondered? 'Phuh,' Masha let out some kind of noise of contempt and disgust. 'Now women have the worst of all worlds. They must work and they must look after their families. No, more than that. I think we have three jobs: it is we who must queue for the food.'

So how did she manage with a daughter, a new baby and a responsible teaching job at the University? Wasn't State nursery care impressive? Again this brought a snort of contempt. 'The groups are too big with not enough people to look after the children. They do not care about them and do nothing to play with them or help them to learn.' Masha got around what she saw as a damagingly inadequate facility by farming out child-care duties to helpful grandparents. It seems that the extended family is still a vital part of Soviet life, mothers and grandmothers being the unsung and unpaid heroines of a system which claims total welfare care.

The family/career conflict can be intense for women, especially educated, ambitious women, she explained. 'At least you have a woman Prime Minister, we have no women in the Politburo, and very few in important positions of power. Soviet men are, I fear, very traditional; they consider the most important thing for women is to care for their homes, their babies, their husbands. Perhaps this will change . . .' Still, I was amazed to see the number of men out in the park on a Sunday afternoon pushing big old-fashioned prams, talking to other fathers, many playing games with toddlers. The general impression was of a society that cares deeply for its offspring. Children were often beautifully turned out with scrubbed faces peeking from brightly coloured snow-suits. I never once saw a kid slapped in public.

As the vodka drained from the bottle, Masha talked of love and romance. She believed in both, and was distressed by the high Soviet divorce figures. 'But what can you expect,' she said, always ready to attack her own country but claiming no desire to live anywhere else in the world. 'We live in these crowded flats with thin walls, no room to escape. No wonder couples fight and leave each other.' I suggested it couldn't all be put down to lack of space. America could hardly be said to have the same housing problem, but they have one of the highest divorce rates in the world. Masha shrugged. She didn't know why it was.

Over a dinner of tasty spiced vegetable stew and olive oil French fries, Volodya put forward his views on the marriage problem. 'You see, here it is very difficult to know a girl before you marry her. There is nowhere to go and you cannot make love together. There are always the parents, your brothers and sisters and you can never be alone. I think this is a very important thing to find out before you get married, but here it is mostly impossible.' For Volodya it wasn't impossible. He was quite an eligible male with his bachelor pad, seductive stereo and double bed. But there were other practical problems to consider – like how to prevent the creation of unwanted offspring. There seemed to be a contraceptive abyss between abstinence and abortion, but we skirted around the question and I didn't find out the exact details of family planning Soviet-style.

If my memories of these conversations present a bleak picture of moaning, oppressed citizens then this is a totally unjust image. Just as your average Britons spend half their life wingeing about the weather, the price of potatoes and the falling standards of schools/supermarket service/TV soap operas, so do Russians complain about aspects of their lives. But they are horrified with many stories about Britain and cannot believe some of the things you tell them.

'Unemployment: Is this true? Are there really so many people with no work?' I was asked this question time and time again by people who could not believe that a Government would let something so terrible happen to its citizens. In the Soviet Union everyone has a job, and for the 'work shy' compromises seemed to be available. I met one intensely artistic young man who spoke like a hero from a Dostoyevsky novel and could quote the poetry of Shelley at length. He had found a job feeding rabbits at a local laboratory which paid adequately, occupied him for 30 minutes a day and left him long hours to practise his guitar playing and write songs.*

Others were shocked at the price of some of our basic living requirements. A charming antique lover in Leningrad invited us to his cosy 19th-century flat in the heart of the historic city and told us that he paid the Government five roubles (about £5) rent a month! This was from a monthly income of 600 roubles. He smiled at my disbelief: 'This is quite normal. Most people pay this money. And in England? – How much for a flat in your country?' I told him that I paid about half of my income on rent, gas and electricity bills for a city flat not much bigger than his and certainly nowhere near as atmospheric. It was his turn for disbelief. His gas bill was 50 kopecs for unlimited supplies every month, and the same for electricity and telephone.

Between his grasp of the English language and my grasp of Soviet economic policies we decided that their necessities were cheap but so-called luxury items were expensive. In England, perhaps this is the opposite, he suggested? I said it depends what you call a luxury: our theatre and ballet tickets can be prohibitive but yours are dirt cheap and readily available to everyone. However, perhaps English women would organise a revolution if Crimplene dresses cost a month's wages!

Talking of Crimplene dresses, Russian clothes are not as drab and dreary as we may expect. Leningrad was alive with colours, shapes and a certain kind of style. In a sea of winter coats bobbed an interesting assortment of hats; antique-looking caps, woolly bobbles, bright berets.

Sitting on a park bench, noisily sprawled in front of mock Roman pillars, we met a bunch of Leningrad youths. They recognised our country from the carrier bag, but rather than the 'You English? You want to sell' approach they asked if we knew of Led Zepplin, Pink Floyd, Deep Purple? They were dressed in a fascinating mixture of clothes. Katya, a beautiful 17-year-old with serious eyes and classic Slavic bone-structure, was keen to practise her English and swap philosophies. She explained the group's attitude to clothes ('clotheses' as she

*Under Gorbachev's new, stricter work discipline, this may not be the case. Editor's Note.

called them). 'We do not like these young people who want always to wear Western clotheses. Have they no pride? They beg from tourists and it is very bad for our country. We are proud to be Russian. We wear beautiful old Russian clotheses, but some people think we are a little strange.' Ironically, they looked more trendy than the young Soviets in their prestigious Western sweatshirts sporting three-year-old slogans.

This lot wore grandfather's old tweed overcoat and trilby, baggy trousers and the odd bow-tie. They had a remarkable air of self-assurance, especially considering the average age was about 18, and many suffer continual harassment from the authorities because of 'alternative' youth activities. In a country full of contradictions it didn't seem odd that this group revealed a confusing mixture of pro- and anti-Soviet sentiments. The KGB followed Katya and her friends because they sang Beatles songs on park benches and daubed public walls with charming peace graffiti at the dead of night. They wanted to be artists, poets, hippies, draft dodgers, peace-activists . . . yet none of them wanted to be dissidents.

Most of all they had keen minds, ravenous for knowledge and ideas from different cultures. Like so many people we met, they were dying to meet more English people and find out every little detail of our lives, our thoughts, our impressions of them. 'Will you tell more people to visit here?' said Katya, her serious eyes fixed on mine, extracting a promise. 'It is so very, very important that they know what we are really like.'

Masha Davies
'Russian Ladies'

Masha Davies, born in the USSR and married to an Englishman, reflects on the position of women in the Soviet Union and on some of those she met.

Returning to the Soviet Union after a gap of about ten years, I somehow imagined that the lot of women must have considerably improved – but I was wrong. Consumer goods were beginning to be more plentiful and small luxuries could be found, at least in the shops of Moscow and Leningrad, but the rest was still there: the dreadful pushing, rudeness and extreme exhaustion displayed by women going about their everyday business of living. Perhaps trying to snatch a pair of comfortable looking shoes, not being 'allowed' to try them on because of the endless queue, and very likely ending up with two left shoes or uneven sizes. There are endless examples of these constant frustrations of everyday life.

Being Russian I would be treated as such, or sometimes as a foreigner depending how 'well dressed' I was. This led to my being either 'bawled' at without any holds barred ('touristy' being the magic key to a certain degree of politeness) or shown off as a shining example of 'good manners' to all the other Russian ladies, who poked not very clean fingers into loaves of black bread to check their freshness, the shop assistant not realising, of course, that I understood every word that was being said. I was once recognised as a 'vazhnyi' tourist, in a café in central Leningrad, but all hell was let loose anyway because the waitress in question was at the end of her tether, with her hair glued to her forehead in wet perspiration and legs shaking with tiredness. Her shouts that she couldn't care less whether we were 'angliskye touristy' or Ivan Ivanovich from Vladivostok, ring in my ears to this day. However it all ended with tears and some smiles (mine rather forced, I must admit) plus a nice tray of chai and pirogi. The other 'angliskye touristy', no doubt, wondered what dreadful scandal had been going on.

This brought home to me the exhausting lot of many women doing low-paid, low-status jobs (i.e. in the service industries) who often end up doing a job meant for two, or even three, people. This in addition to having to do their shopping and domestic chores. They may also have to participate in various committees and will definitely want to be the conscientious perfect 'mamochka'. Children often need to be escorted, largely on foot or by overcrowded public transport, to various extra-curricular activities. It is an interesting idea that full employment can have its drawbacks and seems to lead to under-manning, or, in fact, non-existent staff. The famous Tretyakov Gallery sported a notice for weeks on end saying that there were no cards for sale because so and so was 'bolyna' (sick) or simply 'ne rabotayet' (not working).

It is easy to joke about Russian ladies letting their hair down and shaking either with mirth or fury. Even the matronly babushkis will shake a jolly leg at 'dinner dances' – the norm in overcrowded Russian restaurants. But it is no joke when similar women, looking incredibly old and bent, appear early in the morning at the loos of various camp sites. Armed with a handmade, twiglike brush and a couple of dirty rags as the only cleaning aids, they set to cleaning the filthiest and most disgusting mess it has ever been my privilege to witness. (Camp sites are often used by Russian men after vodka orgies – need one say more?) If nothing else, the new Gorbachev regime may work wonders for Russian loos.

One could continue to catalogue the miseries experienced by Soviet women and lament the antiquated methods of birth control or the inefficiency of simple daily shopping. Nowhere in the world is the art of elbow-pushing and queuing so refined as in a busy shop, mid-day, in any big town. But it is also important to stress that women are used to and have an enormous capacity for hard work, and they also find joy in small things which we in the West take for granted. However, as the standard of living is improving in Russia, so are people's expectations. No longer do women want to stroke someone's velvet jacket, just to feel the unaccustomed nice material, or to have a sensuous whiff of French perfume. It needs effort and time and often ingenuity, but they can get hold of decent consumer goods, even though such things as disposable sanitary towels or Dentafix still have to be birthday presents from abroad. Very shoddy and uncomfortable garments, which previously had to be accepted, are now rejected and supermarkets are springing up here and there. The staple winter diet does not have to consist largely of potatoes, black bread, pickled gherkins and tea. Added to this is the tremendous spirit of comradeship which I noted amongst women. Noticing once a group of male shop assistants (a rarity anyway) standing around gossiping, whilst their female counterparts were hoisting enormous loads to and from lorries, I couldn't help exclaiming in astonishment. The women just grinned, rolled up their sleeves a little higher and flexed their muscles. They contemptuously shoved the men out of the way and shrieked delightedly: 'Don't you think we are as good as they?' Well, I had to agree.

DIANA BARRETT

Hilary Wright
My Dreams

Hilary Wright, an artist who lives in Shropshire, travelled to Leningrad with the same group as Caroline Westgate.

My preparations for the visit to Russia (apart from studying the language for five months) had been peculiar, and had, in fact, been continuing for nearly three years. I have always dreamt vividly, and quite frequently had dreams which were telepathic or pre-cognitive. The first direct impression I had of Russia was three years ago when I received a vivid and detailed description of Kiev in a letter from my step-daughter. A week before I received this letter I had seen and felt everything she described in a dream, including the emotional response which accompanied the physical sensations. This was followed in late 1981 by another dream, both paradoxical and profound, which gave me the impetus to pioneer the local Peace Movement instead of just remaining a frustrated member of CND.

In the dream, I was, at first, looking down from a great height, at a part of the earth where two jutting land masses came close together forming a narrow strait. Then I found myself standing on the shore on one side, looking across at the other, which showed blue and hazy across the sea. The pervasive feeling throughout the dream was one of complete tranquility, as if this was how the world ought to be. At the same time, the thought came to me that this was where the two poles met. It seemed a ridiculous and impossible idea, but the word 'polarity' stuck in my mind and then I understood that I was at a place where the two extremes meet. As I looked inland I saw groves of citrus trees, but paradoxically the words 'You are near the Polar regions' kept running through my head. Looking at the sea which appeared so calm and blue, I thought that it must be deceptive, and that the water must be icy cold, so I walked into the sea, to test it. To my surprise, the water was quite warm. Completely mystified, but still experiencing this wonderful tranquility, I walked inland, through woodland, and though I saw nobody I knew the place was inhabited. Eventually I came to a small wooden building which I felt was some sort of sanctuary. It was empty except for a wooden table at one end, on which I saw something gleaming, which turned out to be a very large cross, taking up most of the table. It was not unlike an unusual brass cross which I picked up in Greece, years ago, but this one seemed to be set with jewels, and was pulsating with a life of its own. I knew it was a symbol of life and closely connected with everything I had just been experiencing, and I also knew that I could take possession of it at that moment. But something held me back, and I thought, 'I'm not ready for this – I must stick to my old brass cross for the time being, and my old life.' I didn't want to leave this incredible place and lose the feeling of well-being but I felt I had to, and then I woke up.

This dream was so concrete in its reality, that it made a deep impression on me, and as I was interested in Jung's psychology of the unconscious I spent a long time discussing it and pondering over its significance. However, there was a sequel to it.

About three weeks later I was listening to a programme on Radio 3 called 'Six Continents', a programme of extracts from foreign broadcasts monitored at BBC Caversham. At the end of the programme the announcer made a brief reference to an idea which had been put forward by a Russian scientist, whose name and sex were not mentioned. He or she had suggested that

American and Russian scientists should pool their technological resources and work together in improving the area around the Bering Straits. The warm waters of the Gulf Stream (and perhaps warm Pacific currents?) could be utilised and diverted to flow through the Bering Straits. The inhospitable climate could be improved, the unproductive land made fertile, so that citrus trees would bloom on these shores. The BBC announcer did not seem to think much of this idea, but commented that such a project might at least 'keep their minds off the production of nuclear weapons'. The effect of this brief newsflash on me was electrifying. I had experienced this idea in a dream although I couldn't properly comprehend it.

Since my return, I have read *Journey into Russia* (Laurens van der Post) and was struck with the coincidence of many of our experiences. For example, he speaks of the Russian passion for diverting the currents of rivers to the benefit of both the Caspian Sea and the northern, ice-bound seas. Isn't the idea of diverting warm sea currents just what a Russian would think of? He also speaks of the deeply religious instinct in the Russian people, and their feeling for the land. The cross in the woodland, of my dream, symbolised this for me. I am not talking of orthodox Christianity, but of something fundamental to humanity – call it a reverence for life!

My deepest conviction after the dream, and the subsequent confirmation of it on the wireless broadcast, was that the seeds of hope for peace lay in Russia. I believe that, because of (rather than in spite of) Russia's terrible vicissitudes, and knowledge of tyranny and war.

Early this year, I had another dream which was like a series of flashes from some panoramic film sequence, portraying vast social upheavals. There were comings and goings in streets and buildings, some of which I now recognise as being Russian, and I sat in a strange room talking with a lot of people I had never seen before. I saw scenes of deceit, fear, militarism, and corruption. At one point I was seated in a wheel chair inside what seemed to be a hospital or health centre. Then I realised that the 'Health Centre' was a mask for something far more sinister. A man in a white coat approached me with a hypodermic syringe, and I was filled with terror, and a voice told me 'Just because you do not hate, it doesn't mean you are not hated.' Then I saw and talked to people suffering from genetic malformations, some of whom looked like Polynesians. Some were resigned, others bitter, and one man wearing a clerical collar was cursing and shaking his fist at the sky. The final part of this dream was apocalyptic in its symbolism. At the point where I was trying to receive an important message, my line of communication was cut off by a peremptory and distinctly American voice. I awoke feeling that I had been travelling in time and space.

Of course, all this can easily be put down to my own subconscious fears or, indeed, the fears of the collective unconscious, but one part of this dream, at least, was repeated in Moscow. At the beginning of this dream, I was sitting in a room full of strange people, and every detail of that part of my dream coincided with the gathering in an apartment on our last evening in Moscow: the outlook from the flat, the sultry evening, the heavy downpour of rain, the child on the balcony. As to the other parts of this extraordinary 'sleep panorama' I have only just been reading that some Polynesian islanders *are* in fact bearing children with genetic malformations due to atomic tests in the Pacific. At the point where I was approached with this awful hypodermic syringe, I actually felt I was another person. Possibly this was a sympathetic telepathic experience, as I have had those before in a very startling way. In any case I hope it's not prophetic for me.

Other members of our group had brought albums with photographs of their homes and families, as a means of establishing a 'rapport', but that method was not for me. This decision was, I must confess, due partly to a sense of shame, and partly to a fear of being misinterpreted. How could I show photographs of our large 18th-century house with its antique furniture, and say 'This is my home – see we live just like you', without appearing to flaunt capitalist values. Although in recent years, I have become a capitalist by position, I am not so by inclination and have little interest in or desire for material things. Having been constantly misunderstood in England, I simply brought photographs of my paintings, which have more to do with me than anything else. Here, I had the right instinct, as I noticed that most of the apartments we visited had original paintings round the walls. My own style, I realised would go down better with these people than it does in England.

Everything in Russia had a sense of inevitability, from the meeting with Sasha and the young pacifists who accompanied us down the Nevsky Prospect, the touching encounters in public places, to the frustrating aspects of bureaucracy, and the paradoxes of the system. Although I had not known what to expect, nothing really surprised me. Laurens van der Post said that when in Russia he found his feelings a better guide than thought and I wholeheartedly agree. Although I felt (like everyone else) the guarded, oppressive atmosphere in Moscow, I didn't share the paranoia that sometimes assailed members of our group. When I think of the openness, the calm, and indeed the complete absence of paranoia of the older members of the Group for Trust who know what the score is, I feel both humbled and inspired. Leaving aside the professional pacifists who have laid all their cards on the table, I did get the very strong impression that the majority of the Russian people do care passionately about peace, in spite of the militarism which undoubtedly exists.

The fear of being labelled a woolly-minded (woolly hatted) mystic, makes me hesitate to describe my visit to Russia as a spiritual experience, but I know no other words. I would have recounted the many amusing, touching, disturbing, heart-warming incidents which occurred, but these are better expressed in speech, as I have discovered, Neither do I want to write descriptions of physical impressions, as I can do that better in paint. Towards the end of our visit a certain rather crotchety gentleman to whom I had taken a liking, asked me if we had managed to change the face of Moscow. I do not remember exactly how I replied, but it was something like, 'No, but it has changed mine!'

Since my return I have read and heard a great deal which confirms my intuitive feelings about Russia. For example in a Radio 3 programme about modern Soviet writers, I heard about the nostalgia for old Russia, its religion, village life and folk lore, and the great attraction it had for modern Russians. There is a knowledge that it is not possible or desirable to 'go back', but there is also an increasing awareness of what has been good in their heritage. No society is static, and with a sensitive use of modern technology combined with this 'awareness', we still have the possibility of a 'paradise' on earth. Peter Ustinov wrote, 'The salient point of my Russia is, that I am not afraid of it.' Rightly or wrongly, all things considered, including the KGB, neither am I.

Joan Murphy
Long Live Peace

Joan Murphy is a Russian-speaker and has been visiting the USSR for many years.

I stared down across acres of ornamental gardens as far as the edge of the Black Sea. A place of ice-creams, fun, lilos, pretty girls and hundreds of tanned Russian children enjoying their summer holiday.

'I do. I mean every word of it,' I replied, turning to look into his grey-blue, northern eyes. 'I simply don't believe in retaliation. *If* Russia were to attack the West savagely and with nuclear weapons, I would not want one bomb dropped on Russia.'

Sasha looked down at the tip of his burning cigarette and smiled faintly. 'I think,' he said slowly, 'that you are trying to win me with kindness.'

'No!' I shouted. 'We've known each other long enough for you at least to believe in *my* beliefs.'

It was our second summer of friendship and endless talks in Yalta. Chance, really, since he lived in Kiev, but came to Yalta to work in a kids' summer camp most years. 'People are in a bad shape here,' he said thoughtfully. 'For the first time Moscow has a phone place where people in a deeply worried state about the possibility of war can ring for reassurance.' He sighed. 'Everyone fears a war.'

'There won't be a war from Russia's side, I'm absolutely certain,' I said. I could smell Japanese acacia everywhere in the soft summer air. 'Not after the last one. Look at those people, all so alike, on the beach. Can you tell the British from the Russian holidaymakers? No? Neither can I. Suppose they were all blown into lumps of bloody flesh – could we pick out the good from the bad, the war-like from the peaceful? War is wicked, wasteful and breeds the next war.'

We looked closely at each other in the gathering dusk. 'Joan, you are a good, sincere Englishwoman. But your government?'

I said gravely, my hand on his arm, 'In the end, Sasha, it is goodness that wins, not governments. Your little daughter, Lena, will grow up to be the future of Russia if you give her *your* ideas. Long live Britain, long live Russia, and under the same sky!'

It was sad. Our last evening. He kissed me gravely on both cheeks, and I hugged him tightly. 'Oh Sasha,' I was almost in tears, 'you're such a lovely person. You're like a great Russian bear with the eyes of a child. Take great care of your wife and Lena, and remember, no war, no hatred, at least between us. We must be brother and sister.' He nodded very slowly and kissed me again. 'Goodbye Joan. I will never forget you.'

He walked down the winding paths towards the sea. When he reached the bend, he turned and waved like a crazy man, and clasped his hands over his head as though in victory over war. I stood and waved until there was no possibility he could see me. Suddenly, faintly, I heard his shout: 'Joan, I believe your beliefs. Can your hear? I believe them.' I waved, but from such a distance he could not see me through the trees.

How can you hate a country you love?

*   *   *

I was a summer student at the University of Krasnodar. The lectures were fairly boring, so I used to go along to the Kvban River every single day to bathe. There was the elderly woman who brought her cat to the beach. She would walk carefully into the water, varicose veins snaking up her legs, and gently put the cat into the water. Attached to her by collar and lead, the little animal swam about, encouraged by endearments from her owner. Afterwards, lady and cat sat together, both wrapped in towels, the cat on her bony white legs. She dried the wet fur until it was fluffy and soft, and the creature lay peacefully on newspaper while her mistress sunbathed.

There were two tiny twins there one day. Adorably plump and healthy, they were guarded by their father, a young man in jeans and a bright green shirt. I asked if I could take a photo of his twins, and he was delighted and proud. '*Double*,' he said, as though he could, even now, hardly believe his luck, 'Double!'

I swam, and had conversations with the lifeguards who rowed up and down the small muddy beach. There was no sand, only sun-baked mud, and on the other side of the river, trees, mixed forests, the whole mystery of Russia.

There were quite a number of girls from the university there, as well as ordinary working girls. Most of them had very, very slim figures, and were extremely tall. The older generation, my generation, were, like me, too fat. Some statuesque women wearing the usual bikini, stood with their backs to the ice-cream stall, allowing the sun to trickle like warm gold all over them. Already they were very tanned. It is a Russian custom to *stand* and sunbathe sometimes for a long time.

At the university hospitalities were exchanged between Russian and British students. Salads and cold meats were eaten in small, overcrowded but neat bedrooms. There were night-time high jinks. Young Brits fell in love with Russians, and vice versa. Arms round each other, they prowled the riverside in the evenings, being young, being happy. We were there for over a month, and love easily blossoms in a much shorter time than that.

There were tears and emotional scenes when we left. One couple were actually married in Krasnodar: an English post-graduate student, and a Russian girl who looked like a gazelle. When we returned to Moscow, she refused to leave Russia, although she had permission to do so. They were very much in love, but she was only eighteen and simply couldn't leave her mother. Poor Richard tried (in three days!) to get a job in

job in Moscow, with the help of Russian tutors, but failed. He
flew back to London without his beautiful young wife. Later,
we heard that he had gone to Russia where a job had been
found for him, and that she was expecting a baby . . .

*   *   *

Cruising from Rostov-on-Don up to Kazan – about a thousand
miles. The beauty of the rivers with families camping, swim-
ming, fishing wherever there was a suitable spot. The vastness
of the farmlands, the quietness of the woods. The friendliness
of ordinary peasants who came to see the boat when it stopped
at picnic spots. The gifts of wild flowers and mushrooms, shyly
given by a couple of collective-farm girls, with broad healthy
faces and pale blue eyes. Kazan, with its white crenellated
Kremlin, and marvellous view. I shared this trip with Bill, a
very old friend. He died last year, so it is like a two-week cameo
of 'Bill, happy in Russia' for me.

*   *   *

On Trinity Sunday I went to a large Moscow church.
Everyone was carrying branches of greenery or lily of the
valley. There were twenty visiting priests from Greece and
there was TV coverage. That heartrending Slavonic church
singing! Children sat on their parents' shoulders for the full
three hours. I moved, and was told off sharply by a woman. We
were shoulder to shoulder, hip to hip; the slightest move
disturbed others. Finally I thought I was about to faint.
Somehow, slowly and cautiously, my friend and I got out. A sea
of people was all round the church, singing.

*   *   *

Russian champagne on the pier in the Caspian Sea at Baku.
Dancing in a public garden in Samarkand. Nearly dying of heat
in Bukhara. So many memories of fourteen journeys to the
Soviet Union . . .
    Long live Peace.

Caroline Westgate
Early and Late: Two Leningrad Evenings

'Come in! You're early!' Smiling, Galya stands back to let us in to the narrow hall. Christine and I had climbed the three flights of stairs to the front door of the flat, our eyes gradually getting used to the late evening gloom. Chipped tiles on the floor of the unlit hall, peeling dark green paint on the walls, an iron hand-rail on the stairs, all combined to look seedy and somehow daunting. Balls of grey, fluffy, poplar seeds, blown from the trees in the courtyard, swirled in the draughts on the staircases. The smell of cabbage came from little zinc dustbins on the landings. The door we wanted was panelled with vinyl – someone trying to add a bit of style – and had a spy-hole. We rang, nervously.

Galya's delight at our arrival dispels all my apprehension. She is in her twenties, slim and pretty, wearing a red apron over her dark dress. She has brown curly hair framing a fine-boned face. Fashionable glasses with big frames focus attention on her lively eyes. She takes our coats and bustles us into the brightly lit living room. Talking animatedly, using her hands a lot, she explains that she'd thought our concert-visit would have lasted longer, and anyway, she asks, however had we managed to make the journey from the Philharmonic Hall so quickly? We'd had a lift? Oh well, that would have speeded things up. Now, there were just a few bits to do to the meal, so would we like to talk to Mark while she got on with it?

Whereas Galya is full of energy and movement, Mark is quiet and still. He is dark-haired with aquiline features and very dark, deep-set eyes. His shirt and trousers are black. In his reserved manner he conveys that he is nevertheless very glad to see us. We sit down and chat to him while Galya is clattering around in the kitchen.

As the conversation unfolds, I begin to disentangle who is who. The flat belongs to Raisa, but she's away for the month in the country with her little boy. We had been given Raisa's phone number by her friend Sergei, a young Russian now living in England, who had asked us to make contact with her, and through her, with any members of his family. Our phone call had been taken by Galya, who is looking after Raisa's flat. She had invited us round, and arranged for Mark, Sergei's cousin to be there.

Galya comes in with a glass plate piled high with cherries, and a bottle of Tokai, Hungarian apricot wine. Cigarettes are lit. The wine is very good, complementing the cherries well. The talk is easy and relaxed. I feel very at home in this room. It's not very big, and rather narrow, with the door at one end and the window at the other. The window is open, revealing the six-inch double glazing. The net curtains don't stir in the warm night air. It's comfortably shabby and the furnishings are haphazard. There are two big armchairs with turquoise stretch covers, a day-bed covered with a rug, and an oval table with a tapestry cloth. A big TV with 1950s-ish metal legs stands in a corner, contrasting with the antique smoking-stand with its legs of turned wood. There is a shiny wardrobe with a big plastic blow-up toy on top of it. Someone has fitted shelves all along one long wall, not very expertly. These shelves reach right up to the high ceiling and hold quantities of books, some family photos, mostly of a little boy with big dark eyes, and some framed drawings. Through the open door I can see a bike propped up in the hall.

Mark is talking about his work. He teaches painting at some kind of evening institute. He shows us one of his drawings, which sits in a frame on Raisa's book-shelves. It is of a cottage in a wood, done in sepia ink, with wax and wash adding texture to the pen-work. He also lets us see some black and white photographs taken at an exhibition he has had recently. The photographs feature his friends beaming expansively and standing in a row in front of the paintings. What's visible of the canvases behind his mates, looks like abstract expressionist landscapes.

Mark talks of his wish to be an artist. To paint for a living you have to be a member of the artists' union. It's a *Catch 22* situation though, because you can't join the union until you've done acceptable paintings, and you aren't likely to manage that if you can only paint part-time. There are two unions, one for artists up to the age of 32 and another one after that. He is 38 and its harder to get into the senior union.

'It's a mafia,' he says.

'Good or bad mafia?' I ask, thinking of some of the jolly, free-booting, jobs-for-the-boys outfits in the UK.

'All mafia are bad,' he answers, gravely.

I ask if he ever wished he'd gone to England like Sergei.

'Yes, I have wished a thousand, thousand times. But I have ties here which prevent me leaving. Three children, my parents, my wife . . .'

Clearly he feels the loss of Sergei very deeply.

'I am closer to him than to my own brother. We have the same soul.'

Galya brings in the food: salad, with lettuce, onion, tomato and cucumber, garnished with uncurled parsley, all fresh and crisp with a good dressing. There's a small roast chicken, very tender and flavoured with garlic, served with lots more parsley. There is black and white bread.

They give us the foam seat-cushions to make us higher on the day-bed, which is now doubling for dining-chairs. We eat slowly and talk a lot, mostly to Galya now, who wants to know all about our daily life. She wants to take a peep out of her locked box into ours. How much, she asks, would it cost to rent this apartment in England? What proportion of our income is spent on gas, electricity and rent? She's astonished that it's so expensive for us. She is animated but not excitable, listening eagerly to all we have to say. Its delightful talking to her. She still wears her red apron. Between questions she presses us to eat more food.

Galya tells us a bit about herself. She's not married, and works as a cashier in an hotel (not an Intourist one). We ask her about the emancipation of Soviet women. She agrees that yes, they can work outside the home just like men, but they still have 'women's work' to do when they come home. She knows some men who help with the shopping which is such a chore. I wonder how long she had to queue for the chicken and the cherries. We ask about nursery care, and whether the nurseries are good. She says the staff have far too many children to look after, and the children are often ill. It would be better to look after them yourself, if you could, or get the children's grandmother to help. We ask if, for instance, Party members get better nursery provision.

'No,' she says

'Yes, of course,' says Mark.

'No, you're wrong. I know so and so, she's a Party member. Her children go to a nursery where there are lots in the group.'

Mark shrugs. He won't argue. Galya will perhaps want to give us the best impression of her country's arrangements. It's all part of being hospitable. The best for the guests.

At one point Chris asks if they have heard that a decree is about to come on to the statute books which would make it illegal for Soviet citizens to have contact like this with Western visitors. Mark says he has heard of it, but he brushes it aside as if he feels it's another example of government paranoia that needn't bother him. He doesn't see how such a decree could be implemented. Then, pointing to a two-pin socket in the wall behind us, he says, 'Of course, that's a KGB bug.' We all laugh.

The conversation turns to our involvement with the Peace Movement, and out come our photographs. Mark looks at them and smiles, shaking his head. He has a way of pursing his lips slightly when smiling, so as to stop a really big grin coming, looking down as he does so. When he meets your eyes he has a steady gaze, as if weighing you up. Mark says that in the USSR they feel ringed by the missiles of hostile nations, from NATO Europe in the West round to China in the East. Suddenly our 'defence' seems very threatening. The game of nuclear chess looks different from this side of the board. A silence falls.

Galya breaks it by saying firmly that we aren't going to solve the world's problems round this table tonight, so we'd better stop talking politics. She makes tea and serves it in a pretty porcelain tea-pot which has a tiny strainer fitted to the end of the spout. Sweets are served, and a big square sponge cake covered with layers of marshmallow and chocolate. Galya says it's called 'bird's milk' and it's delicious.

We produce the gifts we've brought for them from Sergei in England. They turn out to be pretty inappropriate. He has sent a cassette tape, but they don't have a player, and a digital watch, but it hasn't any instructions and neither Chris nor I has a clue how it works.

Sergei has forgotten already, we don't have technology here.' says Mark, resignedly. We offer to take the watch back and find someone at the hotel to work out how to set it. We arrange to call again with it in a couple of days time. We leave Galya, with warm hand-shakes, and walk with Mark back towards the hotel. It's about 1 a.m. and there are very few people about in this part of the city. We walk one on each side of him, talking quietly. Chris says she thinks he looks sad. We both say he looks better when he smiles.

He says, 'I *am* sad. I am a sad man.'

When the moment of parting comes he is only just not crying. He puts his arms around us both, embracing each in turn, then he grips our arms. A brief word of farewell, and he's gone. Chris and I stand by the wall on the river bank, weeping, After a while we walk a little, arm in arm, still weeping. At last we return to the hotel.

* * *

'I'm sorry we're so late!' Lyuba, Mikhail and Marina rush towards us, beaming, ignoring our apologies, and envelop us in the warmth of their welcome. The four of us had travelled by

metro and tram to the suburbs of the city and had got off
opposite a cinema. Our hosts, waiting for us on the pavement,
show no trace of irritation that we were three quarters of an
hour past the arranged time. One by one they each embrace
each of us, with a big hug and two kisses, overflowing with
delight, seizing us as if to keep us entirely for themselves for the
duration of our visit.

They hurry us across a courtyard to the entrance to their
block of flats. We crowd into a tiny lift, more like a wardrobe,
and Lyuba sends Mikhail up the stairs because the doors won't
shut on all of us. Their living room is big and airy, with a set of
tall French windows giving out on to a balcony. There are an
enormous number of oil-paintings, mostly unframed, hanging
on the walls and stacked against the skirting board! They are
brightly coloured, freely painted, abstract-expressionist in style,
with lots of movement and energy. Crowded on to the top of
the upright piano and on a set of shelves in a recess are dozens
of little sculptures, mostly variations on the female nude. I am
very drawn to them. They have a power that belies their actual
scale, and have something about them of prehistoric, mother-
goddess sculptures.

The artist is Marina, daughter of Lyuba and Mikhail. She is in
her twenties, her dark hair pulled back off her oval face and
worn in a bun at the nape of the neck. She has a sweet, shy
expression. She paints and sculpts here in this room, and has no
lessons, no studio, no access to materials for her modelling
other than plasticine, which is a woefully inadequate medium
for some of her ideas. Some of the models are collapsing
because the plasticine isn't strong enough.

Marina's parents, Lyuba and Mikhail, are in their early
fifties, I'd guess. Lyuba is a doctor. She's short and cuddly, with
greying dark hair, and is wearing a black dress with white lace
trimmings. Mikhail, an engineer, is tall and powerfully built.
He has a high forehead and wiry pepper-and-salt hair. He's in
his shirt-sleeves. Their living room serves as studio, eating place
and bedroom, since there is the by now familiar Russian
domestic sight of a bed-settee covered with a rug. There are
books, a portable record-player, family photos, a child's

drawings, and in the middle of the room a table set in our
honour. From time to time the room shakes a bit as a train
passes in the street below.

We haven't been there long before a big pile of photograph
albums appears, crammed with pictures of the missing half of
the family. Sergei, whose gifts we had carried to Mark, is Lyuba
and Mikhail's son, and Marina's brother. Sergei, his wife Nina
and their two small sons, left the USSR five years ago and, as
far as the authorities knew, they were going to live in Israel. But
by prior arrangement with an English friend they really had
plans to go to England, and there set up home on the South
Coast. Sergei teaches classical guitar and Nina is a concert
pianist. Their third child, a daughter called Ina, was born in
England and is now three years old. Her Russian-doll face with
big brown eyes stares out of the photo album. Joan says to
Lyuba, 'These pictures must bring you great joy but also great
sadness.' Lyuba applied for a visa to visit Sergei for a six-week
holiday, planning to leave Mikhail and Marina behind as proof
of her intention to return, but the visa had not been granted.

We sit at the table, red and white china making it look very
festive. They serve tea, and an enormously rich cake, plastered
with cream and chocolate. 'What sort of cake is this?' I ask,
thinking of Galya's 'bird's milk' cake. Lyuba shrugs. She'd
made it herself and it didn't have a name, so she calls it
'friendship cake'. Mikhail pours some delicious damson liqueur
from a decanter and we drink to 'Peace and Friendship'.

Their thoughts are so firmly with their absent relatives that
Lyuba wants to listen to a tape of them playing. They put on a
tiny cassette recorder which can't do justice to what must be a
beautiful piano recital. Our friends fall silent and sit listening
intently, motionless while the tape is playing. Clearly this isn't
back-ground music. The emotional charge in the room is
terrific, and I feel as if all my English reserve and control has
stopped functioning.

The heightened sensitivity makes us all able to share the
anguish of this close-knit family. After Nina's performance on
the tape, Lyuba says 'And now my Sergei, he play for me. It is a
serenade for his mother.' A light but warm voice sings to a

guitar, a Russian folk song. The family sits composed, resigned to the separation, but the cruelty of it is fresh to us, and more tears fall.

Presently, although it is getting late, Marina plays the piano for us, Chopin and Beethoven. She plays beautifully, with a great authority which immediately drops from her as she resumes her modest diffidence after she's finished playing.

At length we have to tear ourselves away. Mikhail disappears and comes back with a big cuckoo clock. He pushes it into my arms. 'Take this to my Sergei,' says Lyuba. He also fetches a bottle of champagne which we must drink with him, and a box of biscuits to go with it. Marina gives us a model of a guitarist. There are post-cards and book-marks as keep-sakes for us, and we have some gifts for them. Mikhail gives me a huge double hug, Russian style. Holding me at arms' length, accepting my tears as if they were somehow proof that I really had shared something with them that evening, he says 'I love you'.

We cram into the lift again, and hurry across the courtyard to the street. They hail a taxi, and after yet more hugs, bundle us inside. It's quite a long ride back and we have plenty of time to reflect on the cruelty and idiocy of there being 'borders' between people. Arriving at the hotel, we discover the family's final kindness – they paid for the taxi.

What has passed between us has been much more than merely conversation. We have experienced a simple but profound intimacy that makes a mockery of all that divides us. The openness and intensity of these two evening meetings has made it impossible to maintain our typical English reserve and emotional inhibitions. Russians, so reserved and closed-faced in public, reveal in private an emotional generosity which is overwhelming. We experienced it not just here but in many other meetings, some fleeting, some longer.

Regrettably, many attempts at expressing ideas of common humanity have degenerated into sentiment: 'People are people the world over' and so on. Most of us believe that we, as individuals, have no quarrel with individual Soviet citizens. They want the same things as us – a quiet life and a future for their children. Even Ronald Reagan has voiced such thoughts, which must surely grant them the status of cliché. And yet, when you *feel* that 'common humanity' at first hand, it becomes an intensely powerful experience. A whole nation of people, in all its complex diversity, has been obscured behind the label 'Enemy'. Under that label, caricatures are painted, and that is all we can see. The Soviets, of course, are doing exactly the same thing, only they built a wall, which is cruder. But the barriers we have built are every bit as real as those physically divisive blocks of concrete. Western leaders are fond of pointing to the wall as the main cause of the cold war. But our walls are there too, and they are more pernicious because they have been built in our minds, and we don't notice they are there.

Linnie Baldwin
Newsreel

Russia 1943:

always the war is black and white to me:
the face of grief on a million faces always the same –
skin convulses on the skull,
the scarf sheets upwards to hide the eyes,
and silent moans ice the breath.
The snow freezes.
The heart burns with hatred
for sorrow is too cold to warm the bones
or fan the embers of the will.
The war goes on.
The bread is made from sawdust.

(My son slumbers at the breast,
his eggshell head nestles into warmth of skin.
The face of love on a million faces always the same. Tenderness
    unbearable in the throat.
I am fierce for him.
Inside the gentleness runs the hard line of the hard iron
of a gun on the hip.
I too would kill.)

Women make armaments,
necklaces of shells to decorate the darkness,
pack explosives, impassively, as if kneading loaves of bread.
This we have always done in silent contemplation of emptiness.
There is no choice when things come to this.
'I buried my children. Stick limbs frozen in the grave – dead
    saplings.
My husband has not returned – although I hope.
I eat my ration and
produce the guns that kill other women's sons.
I do what I must do when life is thin and hangs
precariously in me.
The war goes on – the bread is made from sawdust.'

(There is waste here although we do our best.
The ducks eat the crusts – but still the belly swells with too
    much
as the world spins on the swollen bellies of those with not
    enough.
January shrieks at the window.
The baby sleeps restlessly and turns by the hour.
'No war for you precious boy – no killing sticks fashioned into
    power.'
Brave words defy the vacuum of the time.
His soft flesh smells of milk.
His breath is sweet.
His eyes are pure.
Frozen in a still frame – the moment.
I would crystallise it here, but it will not stay.
We are all ghosts
haunting ourselves in unguarded fragments.)

Leningrad starved that Winter.
The wilderness of snow and rubble sustained humanity barely.
The people lived on poetry and frozen air.
When Spring thawed the ice
the frozen dead rose again to perform their last, stiff,
    ungraceful dance

and then were burned.
The children who were left
thread legs
bent twigs
boarded the boats to take them further back
into the darkening East.
'The war goes on forever – dusty crumbs are what we eat.
The bread, the bread is made from sawdust
and the fruits of our labour fall to fertilise the fields for some
unasked-for harvest
or are bullets moulded from cold lead.'

(Wales 1984:
The first footfall of the year.
We perform the ritual for the child –
coal that we shall be warm
torn corner of loaf that we shall eat.
In holy dread –
we burn the coal
we chew the bread.
The war goes on forever – the bread, the bread is made from
    sawdust.)

PART THREE

TOURLANDZIA AND BEYOND

Introduction

'I suspect that nearly all foreign tourists to the USSR never meet a Soviet family in their own home, never shop in an ordinary Soviet shop (there are special shops for tourists), never eat in an ordinary Soviet café, never take an ordinary Soviet bus, and generally never begin to understand the Soviet people and the Soviet way of life. The tragedy is that by confining tourists to officially sanctioned excursions, Intourist merely reinforces the prejudices and antagonism of the Western visitor. Far from defusing the Cold War, it must surely provide both sides with more ammunition.'

So writes David Baillie, who contributes the first account in this section, about 'Tourlandzia', which is the Russian nickname for the world presided over by Intourist, the Soviet State travel agency which handles all tourism.

Stepping outside Tourlandzia is a lot easier than many visitors seem to think – it may just be a question of stepping aside, and visiting some of the deservedly famous 'sights' by yourself rather than in the middle of a 'party', which gives you little opportunity for interaction with the native tourists and may be restrictive in other ways besides. It may be a question of visiting some of the interesting-sounding places mentioned in

the more detailed guide-books, but not on your tour programme. It may be as simple as getting on a bus or metro train at
random at a cost of 3 kopecks. Echoing David's comments,
Joan Smith, who went with a group of eight women to
Leningrad and Moscow in 1984, had this to say about the
creative possibilities of disengagement from 'Intourist':

> Losing one's way is possible, as we have already proved on a
> number of occasions, but that has led to discovering another
> common characteristic of these people. Rather than just
> pointing the way or describing it, a local resident will take
> you to where you want to be. It is sad to know that the vast
> majority of visitors from the West seem to assume there is no
> alternative open to them but to go on the many excursions
> arranged by Intourist. No doubt these are interesting, but it
> means they never experience anything of the life and culture
> of the local people. Even the 'evening out' at the ballet or
> 'Folk evening' is by coach and to theatres for Westerners
> only, into which no self-respecting Russian would venture.
> And the smiles on the faces of the 'Folk evening' performers
> are so fixed, so un-Russian and staged for the Western
> audience, not at all like the genuine, warm smile which
> breaks across the Russian face like the sun's rays across a
> clouded sky.

> The problem may be that using public transport, poking
> around in shops, sitting in parks, eating in local cafés or buying
> foodsnacks from street traders, is cheap; and the main point of
> attracting tourists, building 'splendid' hotels, setting up 'tourist'
> shops, and amassing fleets of coaches, is to bring as much
> foreign currency into the country as possible.

> So if tourism is for the rich, I'm glad to be poor. We eight
> women are not the only ones to do our own thing; a few other
> people from the hotel are giving the tours a miss, including a
> Yorkshireman in his seventies who spends each day exploring
> the city by bus, tram or trolley bus, putting his 3 kopeck piece
> into the slot, getting his ticket and staying on to the end of the

line . . . wherever that may be. He has had some incredible
adventures.

If you want to relinquish the handrail provided by your guide,
and go walkabout alone in the Cyrillic maze, you will need
some simple aids to self-reliance. This section of the book is
designed to be a kind of 'self-reliance manual', drawn from the
personal experience of those whose curiosity had led them
astray.

The more preparation you do by reading about Russian and
Soviet life and history and the more language you can learn
beforehand, the more rewarding your precious hours are likely
to be. Good, detailed maps (such as Falk maps) and a modern
conventional guide-book are invaluable aids and should be
bought before you go, as you cannot be certain of finding either
once you are there. A phrase book is another item of
equipment which, while not indispensible, will extend your field
of possibilities. Talking to others who've recently visited is
another useful way of getting some topical tips. The point is that
despite the efforts of Intourist to create a kind of tourist
archipelago within whose cocoon the visitor may experience
'normal' touristic sensations such as might be obtained, say, on
a Spanish beach or in a 'Holiday Inn', the country as a whole is
not meant for 'consumption' in this way. So complex is the
psychological and geographical land beyond Tourlandzia that
the importance of sound preparation can hardly be overstres-
sed. Your immersion must begin here, in libraries and
bookshops.

This section also includes a chapter on the question of 'black
market' exchanges and the gift-exchange tradition which
invariably marks social encounters and for which the visitor
needs to be suitably prepared. We felt this was an area
inadequately covered by most conventional guide-books, which
simply warn the visitor not to do anything illegal. The problem
is, that for people who want to make personal contact with
Soviet people, many questions are likely to arise over trans-
acting, gift-giving, and the boundary between these two
activities. We can't supply clear-cut answers, because it's not a

clear-cut area, but we can at least relay some experience which might prove useful.

No disrespect is meant by our lack of emphasis on the more conventional 'sights' and places visited by tourists. The purpose of this book is to help those who want to discover something of ordinary Soviet life for themselves. This means noticing the unremarkable, rather than standing awestruck before the spectacular! This is why Red Square at night, St Basil's cathedral, and so on are mentioned only *en passant* in this book, if at all. We are deliberately trying to shift the priorities of the majority of visitors, who bemoan that 'sightseeing' left them no time for wandering and mingling.

The following three accounts are by those who wandered and wondered under their own steam. In the words of the intrepid David Baillie, whose story follows: 'The sights? Certainly, if you have time after meeting the people!'

David Baillie
No Party:
The Rewards and Perils of Going it Alone

I could write pages about Intourist . . . it's a sort of gothic, Stalinist, Fawlty Towers. Its one role in life is to fill the Kremlin's coffers with dollars, Deutschmarks, sterling and other capitalist tokens. It therefore only caters for the rich and, ironically, bourgeois package tourist who, as usual, has no imagination and expects to be whisked around, ticking off the sights with the least possible contact with the ordinary people and culture of their host society.

Intourist's other problem is that, like all other State organisations, it operates in a different universe where time passes more slowly than in the real world. Intourist is still living through the Purges. From the colourful Moscow street of the 80s one enters the gloom of an Intourist hotel of the 30s. They have to be the most revolting, depressing, and frustrating places I have ever paid for the privilege of entering. Everything is in the most appallingly bad taste, the bureaucracy is indescribable, and nothing ever seems to work. Fittings on the wall have a habit of falling off when you look at them; when you reach to pick them up they invariably break and you can't even throw the pieces away since, like curtains and plugs, Intourist hasn't yet heard of waste bins. In the middle of all this mind-boggling incompetence sits a faulty and extremely ugly TV. Sometimes

Intourist bad taste is so staggeringly awful that you just feel like sitting down and throwing up all over it – only there probably won't be a chair.

When you try to escape from this tourist gulag, you soon find that Intourist cannot cope with the concept of 'an individual'. For Intourist the world consists of Parties. Not political Parties, but coach Parties, and all they want to do for you is organise coach trips – the dreaded 'excursions'. (I've been told that my three weeks spent here in the USSR without going on any Intourist excursion may be a world record.) Intourist cannot handle those who refuse to take part in these dreaded 'excursions' and they had their revenge every time I left a hotel for the railway station or airport: they inflicted the even more dreaded 'transfer'.

The basic idea of a transfer is to get you from, say, your hotel to the airport, with the least possible contact with ordinary Soviet people. A typical transfer goes something like this. You present yourself (as requested) about three hours before your flight, to the Intourist desk at your hotel. There is no one there. You complain to the receptionist desk. They pretend not to speak English. You go back to Intourist. Someone arrives. No, she only deals with the theatre tickets, the transfer person is out.

'Will she be long?'

'No.'

'How long?'

'Don't know.'

'Then how do you know she won't be long?'

'There is a problem.'

This is the one English phrase spoken fluently by all Intourist staff. Judging by the expression with which it is spoken, it roughtly translates from the Russian, 'Listen, this is a sodding awful job, I haven't a clue about your miserable transfer, so will you please shut up, Comrade.'

However, you then parry with the ultimate anti-Intourist attack – 'OK, I'll get a bus.' Instant action! All at once Intourist staff are grovelling at your feet. Even the theatre ticket commissar offers to take the rucksack off your back whilst

another introduces you to Guide No. 1. She/he says 'How do
you do? . . . did you see the Museum? . . . isn't the lake
beautiful? . . .' etc. They escort you to the waiting car and open
the back door for you. You escape from further pre-recorded
interrogation by getting in the front. Two minutes later you're
wishing you'd sat in the back seat after all as the driver (just
back from driving armoured personnel carriers in Afghanistan)
tries to get himself invalided out of both the army and Intourist.
Fortunately the oncoming lorries miraculously fail to oblige and
you eventually reach the airport.

Introduction to Guide No. 2. She/he says 'How do you do?
. . . did you see the museum? . . . isn't the lake beautiful? . . .
where is your Party?' I have no Party. 'No Party!' I'm never
sure which is worse, not being a member of the Communist
Party or not being a member of a coach party. Anyway, after
indescribable rituals with little rubber stamps and meaningless
slips of carbon coated toilet paper, you are ushered into 'The
Room'. The Room is where Parties sit in splendid isolation
from the proletarian masses while waiting for the plane. For an
Individual, The Room has a distinctly empty feel. The nearest
you could get to a party would be a quick tango with the
inevitable bust of Lenin. You escape to the departure lounge
and mingle with the warmth and sanity of non-Intourist Soviets.

Soviet airports are great places to meet people as everyone
seems in especially good spirits. Anyway this welcome break
gives you a chance to recover before a distraught Guide No. 3
('How do you do? . . . did you see? . . . blah, blah . . . etc')
finally recaptures you . After a luggage check you are led out to
the airport bus. The bus then takes you to the plane where you
are introduced to an air hostess straight out of a 1952 *Tracy
Annual*. You glance around half expecting to see Biggles
climbing into the cockpit, while the bus drives all the way back
to pick up everyone else. Needless to say this ritual is designed
to convince your fellow passengers that you have a particularly
unpleasant disease, which in turn ensures that no one sits near
you on the flight. But at least the Transfer Ordeal is over.

There are ways of dealing with tedious Intourist rituals, some
of which I have mentioned above. If Intourist say you have to

go to Leningrad and you'd rather stay in Moscow and you have
some friends willing to put you up in their flat, here's what to
do. Cash in your Intourist train vouchers at the Refund
Department of the State Travel Bureau right next to the
Metropol Hotel. Then get a Russian friend (it must be a friend
since he or she will have to queue for up to two hours on your
behalf!) to buy you an ordinary ticket to Leningrad. This will be
cheaper than your Intourist Rip Off Class so give the change to
your Russian friend.

Enjoy your stay in a real Moscow home, then catch your train
to Leningrad. Avoid disclosing your nationality until the train
has left (not hard if you are going to Leningrad since Russians
will think you are Estonian and vice versa). If the Coach
Attendant looks suspicious put his mind at rest by pointing to
the word Leningrad in your visa. On arrival at your Leningrad
Hotel simply initiate a vastly complicated argument about how
Intourist in Murmansk decided to change your programme,
blah, blah, etc. It rarely takes more than ten minutes to reduce
your Intourist person to premature dementia so you should
easily get away with it.

This trip has been a real education in how to travel as cheaply
as possible in the USSR. For instance, the feared transfer costs
about a fiver, yet the same journey by public transport would
cost about 6p or less. Similarly Intourist meals in hotels will set
you back between £3–£6. Yet one can eat a really good four-
course meal in a Soviet café for less than a quid. Having
thankfully only pre-booked breakfast with Intourist, I found I
spent much of my days in these cafés. They are very
atmospheric places – lots of noise, arguments, laughter (and of
course, chess). In general the secret of Soviet travel is to keep
your contact with Intourist to a minimum. Book a hotel, but
travel everywhere else as and when you please by public
transport. Never eat in the hotel, but venture into the cafés,
grocery stores, or buy from any one of the dozens of pavement
snack sellers with their delicious ice-cream, doughnuts, and
pancakes.

*　　　*　　　*

It is possible for the individual traveller to arrange visits to places other than touristic sights but, theoretically, this is only possible if you do it beforehand through the Soviet Embassy. The obstacles David Baillie met when seeking information about environmental issues do not necessarily mean that his questions were unwelcome. This is in fact rapidly becoming an area of great controversy in the USSR: it is one of the fields where greater openness and co-operation can only be of mutual benefit.

While it may be difficult to conduct free and easy exchanges with Soviet middle management there is no reason why people shouldn't set up visits to places that are of particular interest to them, like David Baillie in the below account. The Soviets may be more co-operative and open in this respect than we might expect.

Ironically, in the middle of this last action-packed week in Moscow, escaping the clutches of Intourist, I spent one day as the guest of another government agency, the Soviet Ministry of Energy. This visit and the ones that followed had been arranged whilst still in England through my Trade Union energy work. The morning began with a long discussion with the Deputy Head of the Central Board of Designing and Scientific Research, and the head of the Foreign Affairs Division. The conversation, conducted through an interpreter, was a fascinating insight into Soviet government, even if it was not particularly enlightening on energy issues! Awkward questions such as the control of acid rain or the disposal of nuclear waste were met with a version of the infamous Intourist riposte, only this time spoken with serenity and confidence – 'There is no problem.' For instance there is 'no problem' with the Atommash plant that is sinking into a bog, and there is 'no problem' with hydro schemes clogging up with silt. In short there is 'no problem' with anything problematic.

I was then shown round one of Moscow's huge Combined Heat and Power stations. It was belching out terrifying quantities of black smoke – 'The Party imposes strict limits on pollution; there is no problem.' Inside, the turbines looked as if they were about to fall apart. There was bent metal, spilt oil,

escaping steam everywhere – 'There is no problem.' Outside
the insulation was falling off the District Heating pipes. 'There
is no problem'.

Soviet energy policy is a subject for a book in itself. However
the basic premise is that big is beautiful, and the bigger and
more centralised the better. Efficiency is not an important
criterion in energy policy. The sight of these huge, dirty, noisy,
and dated plants, often mirrors the lumbering, outdated
machinery of the governmental system which runs them. In this
way my visits to miscellaneous power stations became a useful
tool in piecing together a tentative first analysis of what is going
on in this enigmatic society.

IRKUTSK, SIBERIA: 17th June

It's now been two weeks since I left Moscow, yet I have a strong
urge to return. It is by far the most interesting capital I have
ever visited, yet I hardly had time to see any of its many
landmarks. A morning in the cultural treasure house of the
Pushkin Museum was my only taste of the vast collection of
world art devotedly preserved and displayed in Moscow. Saying
au revoir to a truly magnificent city, I endured a short transfer
and found myself once again on my own among the Soviet
people, on the first leg of the rail journey to Siberia.

En route I spent a day in Yaroslavl. I passed a few hours
taking photos of Polaris and Trident targets. Basically they are
the same as SS20 targets except that, on the whole, they seem
more cheerful and confident. Teenagers in particular seem far
more relaxed and self-assured, especially the young women.
One sees far less of the despairing aimlessness of many of our
own alienated youth. Still, it often occurred to me how a group
of Soviet teenagers set down in a London youth club disco
would be almost indistinguishable from their Western 'enemies'. Only the designer labels on the jeans would give them
away – hardly a good reason for World War III.

From Yaroslavl I spent 5 days on the Trans-Siberian Railway
travelling to Irkutsk. Although I have spent days at a time on
trains in Africa and Mexico, the prospect of 5 whole days on a
Soviet train was somewhat daunting. Each day brought a

constantly fascinating, if slow moving, panorama beyond the carriage window. The train is 13 coaches long and hauled by a succession of vast electric locos that look as if they have been made with a suitable mixture of steel, iron, and the revolutionary power of the proletarian masses – all very stirring. Diesel Multiple Units in England somehow fail to exude the same political and ideological aura of Soviet locos.

It cannot be said that the natural scenery between Moscow and Irkutsk is beautiful, though the ever passing open pastures, birch forests and taiga give a very strong impression of the sheer size and emptiness of the USSR. But there is another complementary, if not contradictory impression, and that it is of the sheer size of the industrial development that has taken place in this 'sleeping land' – the meaning of the word Siberia. Nearing central southern Siberia the view is of mile upon mile of factories, housing developments, chemical works, and the inevitable and hopeless sight of dozens of power station chimneys spewing black acrid smoke into the often smog-bound Siberian air.

Acid rain is going to devastate this part of the world in just a few years; Soviet scientists know it and are commendably concerned. But the inertia of their brontosaurean economic planning machinery means that whatever their good intentions, effective pollution control is many years away on the other side of an ecological catastrophe. One lake in Siberia, Lake Baikal, holds 20% of the world's fresh water, and yet it lies in the path of some of the most toxic airborne pollution on this planet.

In the meantime, life in Siberia is undeniably on a par with many Western countries. Salaries are higher and the population is younger. Having been brought up in the material affluence of the Brezhnev years they demand, and receive, shopping, recreational and cultural facilities which have traditionally been the privilege of Muscovites. Yet traditional architecture, dress, and customs do survive. In Irkutsk old wooden houses with brightly painted shutters nestle beneath new high-rise blocks. Walking around these quiet quarters, with their ubiquitous children's playgrounds and inviting park benches, was the highlight of the few days I spent in Irkutsk and a pleasant way to stretch the legs after five days of exercise limited to walking the length of the train.

I flew up to Bratsk a couple of days ago, to be the guest of the Hydro-Electric Power Department. The dam and generating plant there used to be the largest in the world but have since been deposed by two Siberian neighbours. The flight was in a tiny Aeroflot jet and the pilot made a series of low passes over the dam for my benefit – much to the consternation of the other passengers! Needless to say commuting by air is a way of life in these vast areas and Aeroflot still maintain a fleet of ageing bi-planes to meet the demand for air travel.

The official conversation with the Technical Director of the Bratsk plant was once again blocked by the phrase that seems to have become the creed of the Communist Party – 'There is no problem.' It gets a bit tedious after a while, especially when you are genuinely trying to discover areas where discussion could be constructive. I decided to throw a spanner in the works of their well-rehearsed ritual. In Moscow I had been informed by a leading geographer whom I was lucky enough to meet, that Siberian hydro-electricity schemes were being silted up because of the reduction of river speed caused by building so many dams. However, I told my host that this information had been given to me by Energy Ministry officials in Moscow. This of course caused havoc with the usual protocol. The Director could neither deny his superiors in Moscow, nor could he admit to 'a problem'. Fortunately for him the interpreter came to his rescue and claimed an inability to translate my question accurately.

My subsequent meeting with the Director of the Irkutsk Hydro-Electric Power Plant was far more interesting and frank since he was one of the few Soviet officials I met who recognised the importance of real dialogue, rather than diplomatic ritual, between East and West. Admittedly in our long and memorable conversation conducted on top of the massive Irkutsk dam, we strayed rapidly from energy policy to the diverse subjects of Soviet cinema, 19th-century English painting, Greenham Common, and Tony Benn, but we left with a greater understanding of each other's country and parted as friends.

I'll be sad to leave Siberia – one of the most paradoxical areas in a country of contradictions. I'll never forget watching a traditional Siberian village pass by the train window – rows of beautifully constructed wooden houses all brightly painted; their gardens perfectly kept, with archetypal Soviet peasant women hoeing potatoes in coloured headscarves. In many ways it was the sterotype we have of rural Russia. But it is a stereotype whose days are numbered. Racing down the muddy village street were the grandchildren of these 'timeless' peasants, not on foot, but on brand new BMX bicycles, complete with helmets and knee pads.

Ann Pettit and Other Contributors
Coping With Hotels and Getting On With Your Guide

Unless you book a camping holiday, you are meant to be officially 'accounted for' every night that you spend in the USSR. This means that you can't just cross the frontier by car or on foot, and sleep wherever you like. You stay in hotels, and reports vary as to the stringency of the regime. Some people's absence for all or part of the night seems to pass off without notice; others encounter the fearsome glare of the 'dezhurnaya' (the lady on each floor to whom you are meant to hand in your key when you go out). One way to avoid bringing her attention to what may be a prolonged absence is to keep the key with you. Or you can try staying on the right side of her by being chatty and friendly. Plenty of visitors do treat hotel staff quite rudely, and a bit of friendliness may go a long way.

Moscow seems in every respect to be the least relaxed place when it comes to rules. In Leningrad, during the 'white nights' of the mid-summer season, night-time promenading in the magical, milky light of the early hours is a mass popular pastime anyway, and the visitor who joins in can hardly arouse great suspicion. ('When do Leningraders sleep?' enquired one British visitor, genuinely perplexed to find the bridges and river promenades still crowded with strollers at 2 a.m. Her Russian acquaintance thought for a moment, then replied 'When we are at work.')

It's impossible to avoid hotels completely and for most people who go on organised package tours (the best value for money) you have no choice where you stay. But in case you do want to try to influence where you stay, or just want to be forewarned, here are some comments:

> Book early, go for the cheapest rate then grin and bear it!

This advice comes from David Baillie, who booked, unusually, as an individual through Progressive Tours, who seem to be the best UK travel agents for any kind of individual or group travel to the USSR outside of the standard package offered by the main holiday firms. He adds 'only book the bare minimum, i.e. hotels and inter-city transport, not even 'transfers':

> Big = good in the USSR, but of the two we stayed in, the bigger was the worse – pretentious, and inefficiencies were caused by the size.

I can reveal the name of this establishment – it was the Hotel Cosmos, and was unanimously condemned by all who had the misfortune to stay there. Unfortunately it is Intourist's most commonly used hotel. Another comment:

> Avoid the Hotel Cosmos in Moscow. It's like a battery hen farm with 5000 rooms and it's impossible to get any service – you walk miles from your room to anywhere. But there is a good swimming pool and the bar is a good place to meet foreign students.

The Ukraine, another hotel used by Intourist in Moscow, is described as old-fashioned, with inadequate lifts and water-pressure problems. Poor service seems to be a complaint common to all tourist facilities, except when it comes to guides:

> Our Intourist guides were very helpful and open, and didn't mind when some of us didn't go on the trips or when we asked her to replace an arranged trip with one of our own suggestions.

Any others?,

Besides Intourist, two other organisations deal with tourism in the USSR: 'Sputnik', which is the tourist bit of the Komsomol, the youth section of the Communist Party, and the Central Council for Tourism of Trades Unions. These seem to use different hotels from those of Intourist. A contributor who stayed in the Trades Union hotels found them modern, comfortable and frequented by Russians on holiday, but somebody who travelled courtesy of Sputnik bewailed the lack of the Intourist nannying that irritated others.

Intourist really does seem to try to cater for the visitors who hardly want to do anything for themselves, even down to unloading their luggage from the train and delivering it to the hotel for them. The vast majority of Western visitors would probably feel terrified without the constant ministrations of the ever-smiling, guide-cum-interpreter; those who do want to pursue more independent paths are able to do so, although this is a situation requiring tact if you don't want to appear to be rudely spurning the country's cultural treasures:

We three were part of a party of about twelve; we had our own guide, but every morning at breakfast there were fewer takers for her 'programme' of excursions. In fact, people would compete to get in first with their apologies for absenting themselves, otherwise whoever was last came in for a scolding. I went on one trip just to please her, but it turned out to be the worst one to go on. It was the 'Red Square and the Kremlin churches' one and I don't like icons anyway and I found it very boring. But the guide was nice really and when she saw that you weren't going to do what she wanted, she gave up being severe. We bought her a book of poems from the Beriozka and she positively melted. We would remonstrate that we were having a wonderful time, just tootling around seeing things at our own pace in our own way, but that was obviously not the point: we weren't seeing the *right* things.

Listening to other visitors recount their experiences made me realise how lucky I had been to have stayed in two delightfully old-fashioned hotels which were buildings steeped in historic atmosphere: the Metropol in Moscow and the Europeskaya in Leningrad. Breakfast at the Metropol was a sturdy affair, with excellent fried eggs or large soft-boiled ones, and lashings of stale bread-and-jam, home-made style jam that you scooped out of a big bowl. We found that rather than expecting room service or waiters, you were far more likely to get that cup of tea you craved if you simply went and poured it yourself from the samovar; or tracked down like sniffer dogs the tea-ladies' tiny kitchen in the depths of the building. Here was to be found not only tea, but hours of chat as well.

The bathrooms (to which you needed a key attached to a huge block of wood so that you wouldn't run off with it) were huge with marvellously sculptural plumbing; the dezhurnayas plumped their beehive hair-dos and spent hours inspecting their finger-nails, and there were KGB men, like a pair of fat sphinxes, either side of our door. In short, everything you might expect. But all catering paled before the breakfast feast at the Europeskaya. This was a buffet arrangement, and you could help yourself to a fantastic assortment of traditional Russian dishes, ranging from blinis and kasha to all kinds of delicious salads.

For various reasons, however, a serious discussion of the merits and demerits of Soviet hotels does not belong here, and has little to do with our purposes. We are, after all, trying to encourage visitors not to be fussy anyway and to spend as little time as possible tucked away in their hotel.

Toné Conway
Enemy Images: Taking Photos

Toné Conway, who supplied many of the photos that illustrate this book, gives us his account and another photographer passes on some additional hints.

It is interesting that these contributors disagree on the level of 'camera shyness' to be encountered. It seems fair to point out that most other comments we have received bear out the view of the first contributor, that Soviet people don't usually like having their picture taken as a 'snapshot', and some people have told stories of friendly groups dispersing like snow in summer at the sudden appearance of a camera. Obviously this is a situation calling for tact, sensitivity and communication skills unless you want to feel like some sort of wild-life hunter.

'Intourist' will tell you when and where to get your camera out for views, buildings and awesome spectacles. But what if you want to photograph people scratching behind their ears, or the view from the back of the bus? It is forbidden to photograph bridges or to take pictures, even of innocent landscapes from a train window. It is also forbidden to photograph Soviet missile sites, etc. But is is not against the law to photograph people, it just may not be as straightforward.

It was out of curiosity that I wanted to visit the Soviet Union.

What is it like over there? How do the Russians behave in their day-to-day lives? What is the atmosphere like on the Moscow streets, on Monday morning, or Saturday evening? How do young people spend their leisure time, in a world with no advertising and little fashion, where popular culture has little independence from the state ideology?

It seemed important to travel independently, so I arranged my intinerary through Progressive Tours in London. It took 6 weeks for the visa and coupons to arrive, before I could set off for Helsinki – I was booked from there on the Georgotts ferry to Estonia – with a rucksack, a selection of magazines, tapes and records, and my camera kit. I took a 35mm SLR camera, with a standard, a 105mm portrait and a 28mm wide-angled lens. In the light of the suspicion and occasional hostility I was greeted with as a foreign photographer, I found the long lens indispensible, and I would advise anyone who is serious about taking photos of Russian life to invest in one before their trip. Black and white, colour and transparency films are available over there, of reasonable price and quality, but, to avoid disappointment, it's best to use the film you are most familiar with.

My first encounter with Soviet officialdom was the scrutinising gaze of the customs officer in Tallin. They asked to see what magazines I was carrying, so I showed them a copy of *Socialist Worker* with Solidarity With The Miners emblazoned heavily across the cover page. They allowed me through with no further questioning. An independent traveller is not offered any choice of accommodation in the Soviet Union, and on that first night as I watched the evening crowds thin out from my 16th-floor room in Tallin's Hotel Viru, I was aware of the irony of the situation. Everywhere else I've travelled, from Gibraltar to Guatamala, I have always sought out the simplest accommodation, preferring to live as close to ordinary citizens as possible, but here in the home of Socialism, I was trapped 16 storeys up a 1st-class tourist monolith, uncomfortably separated from my environment by room service and a pre-paid 5-course breakfast.

The following day I boarded the night train to Moscow. I shared a sleeper with an Estonian family, and we passed the evening happily attempting communication, using mime and drawings to tell our stories. Language is clearly a major obstacle, as even the alphabet is unintelligible to the unaccustomed eye. I found that most younger folk know a few words in English, and occasionally French, but the feeling I had was that language education in Russia is as chauvanistic as it is in Britain.

hotel   I was booked into the Hotel Metropol in Moscow, a grand old establishment at the corner of Red Square, with mosaics on the floors and paintings on the ceilings. Each time you enter you must show your red Metropol card to an old man sitting at the desk. Soviet citizens are not eligible to enter, but one assumes they must frequently be trying to do so: hence the old man and red cards. The number of times I was requested to show that card during my week in Moscow, I began to feel like some kind of secret agent entering HQ.

To counteract this sense of being separated off from ordinary Russians I bought a city plan and set off by bus, subway and on foot, in search of everyday Moscow. The result was about 200 pictures of shops and shoppers; crowded bus stops; folk at work; dwellings – modern and derelict; streets – bustling and desolate; and numerous portraits. Some people were willing to be photographed, some were unaware I was doing so; some occasionally invited me to photograph them with friendliness. In general, though, there's nothing much to equal a camera for triggering paronoia, and I soon discovered that in the Soviet Union, unlike in the West, a camera will never be ignored. Obviously the reasons for this lie in the Soviet history. It was explained to me that the Stalinist era was responsible, when a conditioned distrust of foreign reporters plus a desire to remain unknown and therefore untroubled, may have given rise to the almost incredible level of camera shyness I encountered in Russia. In such conditions, however, when one finds willing and friendly subjects, the contact, albeit brief, can be very special indeed.

More tips on photography:

Soviet X-Ray machines at airports, etc. will damage your films, especially high-speed film, so make sure that all your film stock is in your pockets before you enter or leave the country.

Take all film with you. Black and white film is available much cheaper than in the UK but it's not always possible to know equivalent processing times with UK chemicals. Soviet colour film cannot be processed by the standard systems (E6 and C41) used in Britain.

If you take films of 'sensitive' people or places, don't leave the films unattended in hotel rooms, etc. If you have taken some irreplaceable shots then don't wait to finish the roll; take the film out of the camera and hide it in a deep pocket – you never know when your camera may be opened and the film exposed.

Diana Barrett
Looking for Art

An insight into the training given Intourist guides and the way in which the organisation gets it wrong in attempting to cater for the Westerner's expectations, is provided in this account. Diana Barrett, who contributed many of the drawings which illustrate this book, travelled with a group of art students from Reading University with a trip arranged by Progressive Tours, London.

L. lives with her parents in Moscow, and had only recently been employed by Intourist. Consequently she seemed at first to be under a terrible constraint to be very formal with us and drum as much doubtfully useful information into our unwilling heads as she could: heights of monuments, weight of statues, number of trams and so on. But we had not been long in Leningrad before she let her hair down, literally as well as metaphorically, taking the pins out of a hitherto tight knot at the back of her head. She even managed to laugh and joke with us and confessed to a romantic inclination towards one of the students.

Our other guide, though living in Moscow, was a native of Georgia and altogether more relaxed. Right from the start he intuitively gauged the sort of things that interested us, and was informative and helpful answering our questions and arranging special trips. Only when his boss payed a surprise visit, passing herself off as a colleague interested in seeing how her co-worker went about things, but in reality taking copious notes at the back of the coach, did V. become tongue-tied and embarrassed, pouring out reams of statistics, numbers, heights and weights in which he knew we had no interest. After she had left with a cold, bright smile, and her book of notes, he excused himself for his nervousness, and explained she didn't like him. It was little consolation that we didn't like her!

Later that day I was the unwitting bringer of more bad luck for V. I stepped into the road with my camera to get a better shot of one of the beautiful cathedrals in Moscow and ignored, western style, the blasts of a policeman's whistle, thus infringing the rule that streets round the Kremlin are to be kept clear for official cars. V. was reported for not keeping his party under proper control.

With the help of our guides and that of the Artists' Trade Union, we were able to visit two exhibitions of work by practising painters. The first was a mixed show of work in a cellar gallery in Moscow, largely surrealist with a strong fantasy element in most of the paintings. This was memorable chiefly on account of the interest it had generated locally. I have never before been at an exhibition so packed with reverent onlookers. The room was crowded with people shoulder to shoulder, except for little semi-circles of space in front of each picture. They really had come to see the work, not to socialise, and were obviously excited by it. I noticed there were peace themes in the work of more than one painter. The nuclear threat is felt very strongly in Russia.

This theme occurred again at a big one-man show in Leningrad, although most of this artist's work showed idealised scenes of children and animals in a rural setting, the atmosphere heavy with nostalgia. The style was not strictly academic. Liberties had been taken with space and perspective and free brush work. Nonetheless these paintings had no more chance of being accused of modernism than those we had seen in Moscow. A visit to the Repin Academy the following day confirmed that there is no alternative. There, the deputy director told us that in the six-year course 'realism is taught according to the philosophy of our country' and a visit to the life room convinced us of it. The permanent collection of the work of past students had changed little over the last hundred years. Even so, someone had written in tiny letters, and in English, on the back of a screen used for hanging up students coats: 'Free Art'.

I thought about this the next day at the Russian Museum when all our attempts to see the work of the suprematists – those early abstract artists working in the revolutionary years – were doomed to disappointment. At first we were told the room where this reserve collection is held was being re-decorated. Then that the paintings had been packed up for a travelling exhibition. But in spite of a further visit on our last day there and a meeting with the deputy director, we did not manage to see one Malevich or El Lisitsky. Perhaps it is dangerous to rock the boat even with a seventy-year-old revolutionary art in such a vast and delicately balanced social structure as that of the USSR.

One of the greatest surprises to me was how well everything seems to work in a country on such a hugh scale with so many different ethnic groups and cultures. I am amazed at the achievements of this system, from the colossal building projects to the knowledge that everyone has a job and at least a flat that may be lacking in Western-style consumer goods, but has all the basic necessities. I don't think any family in Moscow will die of cold next winter. Nor in Leningrad. And here, if I had conveniently forgotten, the huge cemetry with its long paths cleared of snow and solemn music relayed over the white spaces, reminded me that only forty years ago three million had died in the siege which lasted nearly three years. Would a comparable catastrophe have been overcome in Britain? It was a sobering thought.

Looking at the bustling crowds on the Nevsky Prospekt of well-fed, well-dressed people, the queues outside stores, museums and the place where concert tickets are sold, the serious face took on another meaning. The people of Russia have had centuries of coming to terms with difficulties of every kind, not least that of living in a vast and, for the most part,

climatically inhospitable country and this has had its effect on
their public face. But underlying this there is a warmth of
feeling and a desire for friendship. On many occasions, in the
parks or in a museum, in the hotel lobby or in a shop, people
would come up and talk to us even though we couldn't
understand and had to be content with smiles and nods for our
common language.

After my return to Britain the feeling persisted that I had
somehow left part of myself behind in Russia. This sensation
was akin to that of having briefly met someone about whom I
had previously only heard rumours, of getting to know them
just a little, and being surprised to find them sympathetic and
attractive, and then having to leave before the relationship had
been fully cemented. I want, now, to find out even more about
them and renew that friendship on a stronger basis.

DIANA BARRETT

Ann Pettitt
Sightseeing in Leningrad

I have yet to meet someone who's visited Leningrad and not
loved the place. Leningraders themselves seemed, from my
own limited contact, to be aware that they lived somewhere
very special. 'In Leningrad,' Natasha explained, 'we are
European. In Moscow, they're Russian.' She pronounced the
last word with a distinct curl of the lip. Peter the Great had the
city modelled on classical Italian architecture, on top of a Baltic
swamp. It was to be Russia's window on the West. Here Lenin
arrived from exile at the Finland station, to be greeted by his
fellow Bolsheviks, already half-way to power. Petrograd was
then the capital; maybe some of the intended cosmopolitanism
of its founder survives, for visitors seem to find it easy to reach
Leningrad's Western-oriented youth:

For the centre of Leningrad youth culture with its attendant
fashion, music, drugs, etc., goes to the café on Nevsky
Prospekt under the Moskva Restaurant. It's known locally as
the Saigon. Nearby you can see some of the best illegal
pacifist graffiti in town. A similar hip scene can be found at
the Café Rema.

As with Moscow, the Falk map makes direction-finding easy.

Most people seemed to find the Metro easy to use and the hotels more sympathetic than their Moscow equivalents. The buffet at the Europeskaya is open to (Western) public for lunch which costs four roubles and is very good. The Museum of Ethnography of Soviet People is a must and not on the tours says one visitor (get directions from your Intourist Service Bureau) and another offers this suggestion for a walkabout:

> Your visa does not allow you to go very far out of town, but you can easily go to the area immediately outside the city. Go to Komsomolskaya Metro station at the end of the line and explore the area on both sides of the railway line (there is an underpass). On one side there is a village, with church, cemetery, war memorial, shop, houses, etc. On the other you can also walk through quite a complex landscape, with factories in the distance.

A lovely day out can be had by getting on a bus which takes you out along Primorski Prospekt which leads out of the city and along the Baltic coast. This is the main road to Vyborg and Finland. You are soon out of the city and going through dacha country, a beautiful forest with the beach a short distance on your left. Stay on the bus for twenty kilometres or so, or until you like the look of it, and just get out and walk – there is a path going parallel to the road through the forest, and plenty of paths to the beach. If you walk along far enough you'll come to a little 'shashlik' restaurant which is delightful. This is obviously a popular Sunday outing for Leningraders, yet the forest didn't seem crowded or littered. Primorski Prospekt is a left turning off Kirov Prospekt, which starts at the Kirovskii Bridge over the Neva, on the right of the Peter and Paul Fortress as you see it from the Summer Gardens.

There are two 'sights' in Leningrad which are universally recommended as a 'must': the Hermitage and the memorial to the victims of the siege of Leningrad. They are visited by huge numbers of Soviet as well as Western visitors; but if you are always in the middle of a 'party' shepherded by a guide, you won't get much opportunity for interaction with the native tourists – and you'll also be paying more for being hurried along when you might like to take your time.

If you've spent all your time in Moscow talking with people in their flats, evading the KGB and getting lost on the Metro, then take at least two full days off for a bit of selfish tourist sighteeing, like Caroline Westgate in the following article. It's an unimaginably beautiful city. And don't forget a night at the Kirov Ballet.

DIANA BARRETT

Caroline Westgate
Leaders Old and New

The Hermitage is the biggest art gallery in the world. The queue outside is pretty big too, stretching down the steps from the entrance, along the length of the blue, white and gold façade, around the corner and down the side of the Czar's Winter Palace. There's no special attraction today, no Tutankhamun exhibition. It's just the regular collection of treasures, which always attracts crowds this size. The people in the queue are Russians. The foreign tourists arrive in their coaches and go straight in, marshalled by their guides up to Impressionist galleries, where they are told that they have 'fifteen minutes to see the pictures'.

We have come to the Hermitage without a guide. We came part of the way on a tram, rattling along through the back streets, pressed close to the other passengers. We passed our three-kopeks fare down to the person nearest the ticket machine, who put the coin in for us, got the ticket out and passed it back. We got off a few stops too soon by mistake, and walked through the Summer Gardens. It had just rained, and the tree trunks, grey yesterday like trees in a Pisarro landscape, were black today against the fresh green grass.

The queue for the museum moves quickly. There is a family party behind us: a man in his forties with a mouthful of silver teeth, an older woman in a brightly coloured dress, who is probably a grandma, and two little children. We share some chocolate with them, and get into conversation with the adults. The man is called Sasha and he used to be a sailor. He once put in to the Tyne and laughs with recognition when Joan produces a post-card of the Newcastle bridge. He has 'ten thousand English words' but no grammer to string them together. 'Mrs. Thatcher – Iron Lady', he says, and when we laugh and nod he adds, 'Reagan, good actor', and taps his temple in the international gesture for dumb-head. We laugh some more. Then he points at us. 'Your country, free speech. Here . . .' and he makes his two index fingers into the shape of an X. At this, grandma gives him a shove. Her stream of Russian evidently means 'Shut up, you idiot'. At all events, it's the end of the conversation.

In the entrance lobby there are maps to help you find your way round the treasure-house. We leave our coats and bags, and buy a ticket. It is one rouble to get in (about £1). If you go with your guide it costs £5 sterling, including the coach. We turn into the first gallery. It's stunning. Gargantuan fluted pillars soar up to a painted ceiling. The pillars are gilded, the ceiling richly painted. There's a marble staircase, the steps elegantly shallow so you could walk up in a long dress. Massive chandeliers dip their crystal far above our heads. Tall windows look out on to the neo-classical sweep of the Palace Square, yellow and white colonnades, and a triumphal arch topped by six massive, bronze horses pulling a chariot. In 1905, against that magnificent backdrop, the Czar's soldiers gunned down a crowd of peasants who had come to ask the Emperor for more bread.

One gigantic gallery leads into another, each as magnificent as the last. There are six-foot-tall malachite urns of an improbably rich viridian green; carved wood panelling reaching up to intricate moulded ceilings, polished marquetry floors, carpets, tapestries, statues and pictures, pictures, pictures. The crowds, moving slowly through these outward signs of the Romanovs' supreme power, talk in hushed tones. One of the attendants rebukes us firmly but politely because we're laughing at something. There are a lot of older people with youngsters. Perhaps they are grandparents telling their grand-children how, as children themselves, they were lifted up to see the Czar's carriage drive past. There are some benches and red velvet upholstery and gilded arms, and these are crowded with people resting their feet and thinking their thoughts. Perhaps, like me, they're thinking that the Romanovs asked for all they got . . .

The Impressionist gallery is magnificent. Here are paintings I've wanted to see since I was a teenager, plus a whole lot more that I've never seen reproduced in the West. It's maddening that there are absolutely no prints or post-cards on sale, just a few unbelievably expensive coffee-table books. There are a few people taking photographs in the galleries, with big tripods and plate cameras. You'd only need to flog a few negatives to Thames and Hudson and you could finance your whole trip.

We suddenly realise we're really hungry. (Being merely peckish wouldn't be enough to make me leave the pearly-lustre of the Degas pastel, or the daylight spilling out of the Manet.) So, where can we get something to eat? Downstairs there are two places – a café and a buffet. There are queues for both. We decide on the buffet, and stand around outside a pair of tall doors which are shut. From time to time a few people, who have finished their meal, come out, then the doors close again. After about ten minutes a burly woman in a whitish overall opens the doors and the queue surges forward. A few get in, fifteen perhaps, and the door shuts in the faces of the rest of us. This happens three times, and each time we fail to get in. It dawns on us that when the doors open people are rushing forward out of nowhere and pushing in ahead of us. How un-British. We form a cunning semi-circle in the queue, enclosing the door, so that shoulder to shoulder we can press forward into the buffet when the door opens and no one can get in ahead of us. This neat manoeuvre works, and we find ourselves, next time the door opens, inside a large, square room.

There's no light on, and it's very gloomy because there's only one window in the corner. What's more, after all that waiting, there doesn't seem to be any food. Close inspection reveals that there are Frankfurter-type sausages on sale behind the counter. The big woman who is in charge of the door is also dishing up the food. You tell her how many sausages you want, she picks the pale, rubbery things out of a vat of cloudy hot water, puts them on a paper plate, weighs them and tells you how much to pay. You help yourself to black bread cut in slices and arranged on an enamel tray. To drink, there's brown fruit-juice ready in glasses. It looks unappetising to Western eyes used to lurid food colouring, but it tastes good. For some reason they're selling boxes of chocolates here. People are buying them six or so at a time. Apart from that there are only oranges on sale.

We take the food and squeeze round a small table. We watch everyone else tucking in to the bread and sausages. It tastes better than it looks. This is the Soviet equivalent of a fast-food joint. People here are eating quickly and aren't talking much. Just filling their faces before getting on with their afternoon in the gallery. After a while the tall doors fly open and a great surge of people bursts through. The woman in charge of the sausages tries to shoo them out again. Voices are raised. The poeple who have got in are staying in. The woman shrugs and goes back behind the counter. How can she deal with the food *and* organise the queue? With no good grace she bows to the inevitable. Someone appears with two more enamel trays, piled with ham on slices of bread. It looks good, better than the sausages. But it's too late now. The pictures beckon again.

We stay till closing time. On the way home we cross a pretty cast-iron bridge over one of the innumerable canals. Some workmen are meticulously gilding the gryphons whose wings support the span. I try to make sense of the swirling kaleidoscope of the day. One of the paintings we'd seen showed a Bolshevik taking the red flag from the hand of his fallen comrade. His eyes were blazing with determination and idealism, and he looked strong enough to fight through to victory. There was great dignity in his figure, as he seized not just his flag but his own destiny.

But today, what freedoms do heirs of those heroes actually enjoy? Our friend in the queue mentioned the lack of freedom of speech, in the course of a ten-minute conversation. If that topic comes up during the brief chat that passes the time of day, I'd guess that was because it's pretty close to the heart of the speaker. On another occasion, an elderly woman came up to us as we walked the street, stopping us with the greeting 'Hallo, pretty girls!' We talked to her for perhaps three minutes. 'Leningrad is a beautiful city,' we said. She replied 'Oh, yes, beautiful, but . . .' and then she turned her head slowly to right and left, as if looking for someone who might be taking note of what she was doing.

When the ruthlessly powerful Czar was overthrown, the gilded halls of his palace were open to ordinary citizens. They throng the place now, enjoying the treasures and seeing for themselves the obscene splendour in which their former oppressor lived. When the liberated Soviets queue up for lunch, they can reflect that it's undeniably better to eat indifferent food inside the Czar's palace than be shot for asking for bread outside it. But afterwards, if they cross the gryphon bridge on the way back to their cramped flats, those citizens may ponder whether the city fathers who ordered the gilding have got their priorities right. And I've a feeling that if the Bolshevik in the painting came back to life, he'd reckon that, when it came to throwing off oppressors, there was still a fair bit of it to do.

CAROLINE WESTGATE

After a few false starts Caroline and her party finally established that Bus no. 50 went to the Siege Memorial.

We approach the memorial down a wide road, and walk round it because we wrongly assume an underpass won't take us to it. I sit on the grass and draw it while Hilary and Joan have a fag. Decide I really can't like this heroic sculpture – vast groups of figures flank a truly massive red column, which from this angle dwarfs a sky-scraper behind it. Joan says there aren't enough women in the statues, considering they suffered along with the men, but there are more on closer inspection – mother saying farewell to her soldier son, a nurse, a woman casting shell-cases.

We finally make it to the memorial via the underpass. It had better not be an anticlimax after all the trouble getting here. It isn't. A huge broken circle encloses a statue of a group of sorrowing people including a woman holding a dead child. Rachmaninov's second piano concerto, playing from some hidden speakers. Flames, flickering in torches. 900 days, 900 nights in gold lettering. We put our flowers with the others at the statue's foot. A wedding party comes and the bride puts her bouquet on too. They stand still for a second or two looking serious while they have their photographs taken. The people with the bride and groom have red sashes diagonally over their shoulders and the wedding car has red pennants.

Down below this is a large, low-ceilinged room with display cases bearing relics of the siege – the 250 gm of black bread and the diary of the little girl laconically recording the deaths of her family one after the other, ending 'the Savichevs have died. They have all died. Tanya alone is left.'

A large screen in an alcove at the side shows clips of film shot during the siege, edited together with no sound track. Great guns belching shell after shell, people digging trenches in the streets, the troops marching, winter coming and the famine taking its toll. A fleeting glimpse of a woman keeling over in the street and being helped up. She falls and is lifted up again completely stiff, like a dummy. Her face reminds me of the Picasso I saw yesterday – completely motionless, mask-like, suffering personified. Perhaps she was dead already.

   Down the corridors to this hall and all around its cornice are 900 flickering torches. Large mosaics at the end depict the siege, and there's a big relief map to show where the Nazis were. Incidentally, they never refer to the 'Germans', always the Nazis or the Fascists.

   It's impossible not to react to this museum, and interact. It's like being in the belly of the whale, swallowed up in this dark, enclosed space. Back up in the sunlight, past the attendant's room where something a shade lighter than Rachmaninov's second is belting out of a tranny, the heroic sculptures of the defiant Leningraders tower above us. Somehow the tiny piece of bread conveys the suffering more than the mighty obelisk and the bronze figures. The official expression of the pain is on such a huge scale that it's hard to identify with it. One person can only feel one person's grief. One million people died.

Masha Davies
Camping in Russia

Most people go first to the two main cities when they start to visit the USSR, and tours tend to spend longest in them. If other places are included in the tours, this tends to be as part of the rush to include as much as possible in a week or two, and it's obviously difficult to develop any personal contacts when you may only spend two days in each place.

The Soviet Union is so huge and varied, with so many races and cultures, it seems crazy just to try to 'see' it in dollops of two days here, two days there. It would seem worth more people trying to form groups to visit, and then negotiating their own special intineraries with Intourist, in which they would stay longer in one place and have more chance to get to know people and to understand the culture.

The vast majority of travel in the USSR seems to be city based. Hardly anyone from this country ventures to travel about rural Russia. 'Can you go camping?' people ask. The answer is you can, so long as you organise it beforehand. Masha Davies, who supplies us with the following account, is a Russian married to an Englishman.

Like many other people, the thought of having to book one's trip in advance, pre-pay and prepare an itinerary over unknown

territory in East Germany, Poland and the Soviet Union made
my husband and I hesitate for several years before we finally
'had a go'. The journey was made in 1981, because we found
out that there were 1981 miles from Liverpool to Moscow. We
couldn't resist such a coincidence!

The first step was to write to the East German authorities,*
and Intourist. It did not take very long, and the documentation
was not too long-winded or complicated. We sat down with a
good map, diary, pencil and paper and sketched out a fairly
rough itinerary, asking the various authorities for guidance as
regards recommended mileage and comfortable distances per
day. We found everyone very co-operative and we agreed to all
the stipulated 'money in advance' payments, etc. We opted, at
all times, for the very cheapest possible camping accommodation, always afraid that we might not manage to get there at all
and lose our money paid in advance.

As the rules and regulations change from year to year, there
is no point boring everyone by probably giving the wrong
information. I can only stress that foreign motorists are
welcomed and the authorities are helpful. We need not have
feared that rigid adherence to our schedule was essential. If the
car breaks down, or there are other hold-ups, the itinerary can
be changed without too much fuss. We found to our delight that
the camping accommodation was good and by paying extra
(usually in the local currency) to the camp authorities on day of
arrival, we could change to a hotel room, if we were really
exhausted, or rent, very cheaply, a small 'domik' (hut/
bungalow, containing basic furniture for two and often cooking
and washing facilities). The 'domiki' were particularly splendid
in Moscow and Leningrad.

The initial planning was probably the most daunting task and
in retrospect it was all fairly quickly and smoothly accom-
plished. Once we were on our way, our nervousness gave way
to delight and a sense of adventure in discovering the lovely
countryside and meeting ordinary people in ordinary, everyday,
real-life situations. We also became friendly with fellow

*via Berolina Travel Ltd, 20 Conduit Street, London W1. Poland: Polorbis, 82
Mortimer Street, Regent Street, W1.

travellers. Alas, not many English! As the same routes are prescribed for all motorists you *do* bump into one another (some even literally on the rough roads!), exchange gossip particularly about road conditions and give, or receive, help if necessary.

Although we were labelled 'dikiy touristi' (wild travellers) we felt sometimes bewildered but certainly not 'wild'. We were just enjoying absorbing the country at our own pace and trying to fathom out the Russian (or indeed Polish, and East German) way of life. We were often very touched, amused and sometimes exasperated. Our first meal in Moscow was fairly typical of the kind of Gogolian 'laughter through tears' that we learnt to accept. Pelmen'aya – a restaurant *specialising* in pel'menyi – a type of ravioli, either sweet or savoury – sported nothing but fried eggs. The pel'menyi were *off*, no explanation given, but three fried eggs (neither less nor more) were *on*. Being hungry we grabbed the eggs and some black bread, but were was the cutlery? After a lot of grumpy grunts a couple of aluminium table spoons were produced and we had fun eating our dinner in the great metropolis!

We discovered delightful, hidden ponds or rivers all along the country routes, not to mention a very Russian fishing/boating/ paddling scene in Brest-Litovsk, where we could have a quick dip, either in splendid isolation or with one or two onlookers urging us not to go too far out.

There were of course moments of panic and sometimes frustration. The procedure at the customs was tedious, but perhaps we were just unlucky. It was no joke emptying one's car completely, with customs officials suspiciously prodding sleeping bags, examining tent pegs and dissecting bits of the car's interior. There were problems in finding reasonable meals; we were 'dikiy' after all, and didn't fit neatly into the organised package-tour parties and their prescribed three-course dinners. Finding road signs and the correct turnings proved awkward sometimes and, above all, the ability to speak Russian was a definite bonus. A grumpy 'nyet' would soon give way to a smiling 'of course' if one could communicate in the language. Potentially nasty incidents were resolved in kindly smiles and much cheerful waving.

Talking of roads, they were pretty bad – even the good ones. Polish petrol was horrible and one shuddered to think what it did to one's car engine. Two star petrol was fairly luxurious – most grades seemed well below that kind of grading. Petrol coupons helped, particularly in Poland. The so-called motor-ways have potholes, not to mention suicidal chickens and horses and the odd little lady out on a sunny stroll. Speed limits seem arbitrary, but one wasn't really tempted to go fast. Neither is it advisable to drive after dark. Road checks are very frequent (these are *not* confined to foreigners) and here again a cheerful smile and a little Russian worked wonders.

It helps to have good maps. The AA supplied us with a reasonable through-route and we had the usual Green Card and recommended insurance cover (luckily, we had no motoring mishaps the whole time). We found Russian road maps helpful and Collet's* may supply motoring maps too. It is important to stay on the prescribed route, but if you really go wrong, just try to find your way back to 'your road' again. Don't make the mistake of asking the local motoring police – they are supposed to arrest you, if you are in the wrong area.

This happened to us and it caused a lot of unnecessary delay. After taking the wrong turning on our way from Leningrad and finding ourselves in rather military looking territory, we were foolish enough to stop a GAI official (in theory the organisation for helping out motorists). After some humming and ha-ing it was finally decided that we had committed a crime and had to sign a formal statement to that effect. On noticing my husband's irate comments in English, the tone of the 'interrogating' GAI cum-military became visibly more belligerent. Not understand-ing English they had to accept my deceitful explanations that my husband was shouting because he was hungry and I had been a poor navigator. My explanations were accepted very grudgingly with many suspicious looks at my lawyer-husband, who was in fact insisting on being properly represented and refusing to sign statements admitting our 'guilt'. For once, I

*Collet's Bookshop, Charing Cross Road, London WC2.

used my superiority as a linguist and quietly signed, grovelling apologies and admitting all kinds of traffic crimes. If I hadn't done so, I feel quite sure we would have ended up in some delightful prison camp in the depth of Siberia! Instead we just lost half a day and had to start our journey to Finland all over again, taking great care not to lose our way a second time. However, all this would never have happened if we had just quietly rejoined our 'route'.

My husband was particularly struck by the interest shown in our humble Renault car; wherever we went, we attracted hordes of men and boys peering at the rear windscreen washer, right-hand steering wheel, etc., but we never suffered any theft or pilfering. My husband felt that for the first time in his life he could empathise with the plight of a young pretty woman, constantly pursued by amorous gentlemen!

It goes without saying that one should take plenty of emergency supplies and basic camping ingredients. Best of all, take plenty of good humour, a sense of adventure and you will enjoy the discovery of a much more 'real' Russia than you get in the usual tourist travel tours. Russia is a country of paradoxes and I can't wait to set off on another bumpy car journey which may reveal a few more hidden treasures or horrors!

Ann Pettitt and Other Contributors
Survival Briefing

To leave the safety of your party for the hazards of independence, you need to feel able to tackle the public transport
system, and to stay free from hunger pangs. Any degree of
language is a confidence booster; our Appendix on Russian
phrases is not intended as a substitute for a phrase-book, but we
try to include a few of the most useful phrases that might assist
the adventurous. Knowing the Russian alphabet does help
(Appendix 1).

Next to language, the most liberating thing you can have is a
good map. Reports vary as to the availability and accuracy of
maps in the USSR. So this really is an important item to buy
before you go. The best available maps are the German Falk
maps, and you can get these from Collet's Bookshop, Charing
Cross Road, London WC2, or Stanfords, Long Acre, London
WC2.

MOVING ABOUT: THE METRO

I think the most striking consensus to emerge from all the
accounts of visits I have read is the admiration for the transport
systems in all the major cities. Crowded they may be, but they
are efficient, incredibly cheap compared to the Western

not
bookings

equivalents and they work on trust: in the Metro and on trams and buses you get your ticket from a machine. Cheating would be easy, but no one seems to and indeed why should anyone? Here is one striking instance of socialised provision for a common need that really works.

The Moscow Metro is justifiably world-famous. It is very fast and the trains are frequent. The stations are spotless marble palaces full of dramatic revolutionary sculptures in a fine classical style – all arches, Corinthian columns and heroic, industrial tableaux. Palaces they may be, but somebody has to clean them. We came across two old ladies pounding down what felt like a kilometre-long corridor, pushing metre-wide brooms in front of them. As they passed, we could hear them intoning a sort of rhythmic chant, which in translation would go a bit like this:

You walk and you walk and you walk,
And you sweep and you sweep and you sweep,
And you gather up the dust, gather up the dust
At the end.

However the Metro is not quite as easy to use as it looks. Put a 5 kopek piece into a slot machine on entry to the station (marked with a big 'M'). Change machines and cash desks are by the entrance. Trains run every three minutes, more frequently in the rush hour. It is sometimes difficult to see the name of the stations from the carriage and sometimes stations which are big intersections have two or even three different names, depending on which level you are on. You can make sure you get out at the right stop by counting the number of stops from where you begin. Also each stop has a different decor and it gets easier, of course, the more you use it.

The 'last train' is at 1 a.m. and Leningrad and Kiev also have Metro systems run in the same way. Metro stations are popular for rendezvous with people, but be specific – there may be more than one entrance, and it may be hard to get from one to the other without buying another ticket and going along the platform and up the other side. This sort of thing contributes to an atmosphere of wild farce, but can be less funny if your nerves are wearing thin and your time is running out.

BUSES, TRAMS, TROLLEY-BUSES AND TAXIS

Buses, trolleys, trams are frequent. Take the plunge and muddle through on the public transport system. Fares are so cheap (5 k. for buses, 4 for trams, 3 for trolleys) you can afford to get on a bus or tram that seems to be going your way and hop off as soon as it turns off your route – then get another.

Street names are rather small so unless you have some idea of the district you want, you could have a problem, particularly in non-Russian-speaking parts of the USSR.

When really crowded (there seems to be no restriction on numbers, just so long as the doors can be closed), money is passed down and the ticket passed back. The word you need is 'peredaitye pozhalsta', which means 'please pass my money down'. Otherwise just put your money in the box and tear off your ticket.

Metro and buses are easier than taxis (these always seemed to be booked when you want one) whereas taxis are best in Tbilisi and there buses are free. Taxis are cheap (metres are on dislay) but subject to driver's whim, as well as complications – some only operate certain fixed routes for example. Here the system works against you, as taxi drivers get paid anyway for their week's work, so why should they take you miles out into the suburbs when they can have a much easier time ferrying tourists around between the main hotels and the central 'sights'. The time of the day makes a difference as well – at night, taxis may be very willing to return you from the outskirts to the centre and your hotel, but unwilling to make the reverse journey. A little, green light signals availability: so why do you stand there frantically signalling to 'available' taxis that just drive past? It seems to be pot luck, and we were lucky enough to have some extremely obliging taxi-drivers who certainly didn't charge the exorbitant fares reported by others for making a trip outside the central area. If you really need to take a taxi as there's no other hope of finding an address you've been given, or getting to somewhere you really want to go, a pack of flashy Western cigarettes, purchased duty-free from the airport, can come in handy. One of you sits in the front with the driver (only members of the Politbureau ride *au chauffeur*) and it also helps to print an address clearly in Russian if you're not sure of your pronunciation.

However, private enterprise does also come to the rescue, particularly outside Moscow, and in Leningrad. This is not an illegal, but a parallel, system, whereby car owners can stop and take you to your destination for the same flat rate as a taxi. So if cars stop and offer you lifts in the middle of the night don't react the way you might in the West – they are trying to be helpful and you pay them. One way to avoid rip-off prices for unusual or longer journeys can be to say the area where you want to go and agree a price beforehand. Many might be keener to be paid in 'gifts' than roubles.

If you find the public transport system too much to face, don't let that deter you from getting out and about. One contributor voices another common opinion when she says: 'Walking is a pleasure – no feeling you're about to be jumped. Russians are good at strolling and sitting on park benches, so join in!'

Most people who travel long distance by *train* comment favourably on the nice old-fashioned samovar-lady at the end of each carriage, who makes you tea; the fold-up comfortable bunks with clean bed-linen, the camaraderie of the journey and the opportunity to meet people; and comment unfavourably on the loos. I would extend this last to include the public loos in the stations, which were quite the most appalling I had ever encountered, despite the presence of attendants.

EATING

Most people agree that the food in the hotels was ample; some were more enthusiastic than others:

Hotels all had very good food, for vegetarians too. Apple juice, yoghurt, eggs, bread and jam and coffee or tea for breakfast. Variations were salami or garlic sausage instead of eggs or cream cheese. Three-course lunches with meat or fish or a vegetable – nut pâté for vegetarians, ice-cream, soup, wine and fruit juice.

Food rather stodgy and dull; very little fresh fruit.

Our hotel provided excellent food and plenty of it. There was a lot of meat and not much fresh vegetables and salad, so vegetarians weren't too happy. Some days it was debased international cuisine (e.g. steak and chips) but it was well cooked and presented, and they did do us 'real' Russian food like *blinis* and *borsch*.

The main problems likely to be encountered are evident just from these few accounts. As one seasoned traveller put it:

You'll get ample food, but rather stodgy, not enough fibre, probably not much fresh fruit and vegetables. This can upset your stomach, lead to diarrhoea or constipation or both, with much discomfort: public toilets are few and far between. and not always very clean. Always carry toilet paper and soap.

Take high-fibre biscuits with you and eat them regularly – this helps. Other fibre-rich foods you can buy there include dried fruit: big packets of apple or mixed dried fruit are called 'sukhoi kompot', and are not expensive. It's plain that vegetarians may be in for a tough time in a very meat-orientated food culture. But here are some 'survival tips' for vegetarians: 'Kholkhoz-niks' are people who work on State or collective farms, but also often have a little land of their own on which they grow vegetables and fruit. They sell this produce in markets which are called 'Rinoks'. Here is to be found a supply of those fresh fruit, vegetables and dairy goods that appear conspicuous by their absence from the State food stores. But they are expensive. One of these markets is by the Rizhskaya Metro station on the line going north from the centre of Moscow. Others are listed in Fodor's guide. One regular visitor says no one should miss his favourite one, which has been renamed a 'Yamaika' (bazaar). He describes it as a colourful cornucopia where anything, from picnic ingredients to cut-price souvenirs, can be bought. You go to Metro Profsoyznaya, then take a bus one stop or walk to the corner of Profsoyznaya and Ulitsa Vavilova, where, he says, 'you can't miss the market'.

An enterprising visitor managed to discover the restaurant which gives you a bird's -eye view of the Kremlin:

Opposite the V.I. Lenin Central Museum at the entrance to Red Square is the Hotel Moskva, usually reserved for top party officials. Near the south-west corner opposite the museum is a typically unmarked grotty doorway which leads to a good, cheap self-service café.

For a more interesting excursion, enter the doorway, but instead of going to the café follow a corridor to the right and find a lift. Tell the attendant 'Kafe' in your best Russian accent (it's not on the official tourist list but if you look as if you know what you're doing you should get away with it!) and zoom up at least a dozen floors to an open veranda leading to a waitress-service restaurant (not too expensive). But the best bit is the view from the open veranda overlooking the Kremlin and the whole of western Moscow.

One regular visitor recommends a Moscow Café and Beer Bar which have been recently restored to their original splendour. Both are on Stoleshniki Lane, off Pushkinskaya Ulitsa and Gorky Ulitsa. The Café is called Gilya and the entrance is in a courtyard beneath an awning. Five roubles entrance buys you a meal!

In the autumn, woods everywhere are likely to be full of Russians foraging for wood fungi, a fascinating pastime with gastronomic rewards. Don't forget to take a bag, or a hat, or something to put your finds into and don't eat anything without asking the advice of a native!

The other answer is to take stuff with you. What about dried soups? Hotel restaurants have samovars somewhere in the corner, from which to refill your tea with the boiling water from the tap. No reason why you shouldn't use it to make up a cup of soup.

Some hotel restaurants advertise themselves as being open during the day to tourist parties. But the doorman may refuse to let you in unless you can wave a piece of paper at him to show that you are a bonafide resident. Tantrums have been used with occasional success in this situation. Other restaurants or cafés may be tucked away, unadvertised, on various floors of the main hotels. Whether the qualification for sitting down to eat is simply time spent in a queue, or whether you have to occupy a special privileged category, seems to be a matter of luck.

To the Westerner used to 'fast food' places, and main roads crammed with competing signs inviting you to feed your face with the Westernised cuisine of a dozen different countries, eating outside of the predictable hotel fare can be a problem. There are street kiosks selling things that look like hamburgers, and for sheer easy fillers, stodgy cakes, sometimes stale, are also to be found from kiosks. The rule seems to be to watch out for queues, and join them if it looks edible. However, the news is that Moscow's new Party boss, Yeltsin, is improving the quality and availability of street-sold food in the capital.

Everyone agrees that the ice-cream is superb; beyond that, opinions vary about street and 'café' food. Some people say they ate four-course meals for one rouble. This probably means that they were lucky enough to encounter a better-quality than usual 'stolovaya' (CTOMOBAP) – a stand-up cafeteria. These places are worth looking for because the self-service set up avoids the notorious long waiting periods of the 'proper' restaurants, while the rock-bottom prices at least guarantee that you will fill that hole, even though you may not be savouring gourmet delights.

Such a place may appear to be an unmarked doorway in an otherwise undistinguished building, the only hint as to the nature of the establishment being the smell wafting from the doorway – a saliva-stopping mixture of over-boiled stale meat, cabbage and disinfectant. If, on peering inside, you see something like high, round, marble topped tables with people standing at them who appear to be eating at a great rate of knots, then you have found a stolovaya. There are plenty on Gurkvuo Ulitza.

On the occasion of my own visit, overcooked rice and pink and grey sausages, and a very watery, greasy soup enlivened by the odd cabbage leaf – the famous 'shchee' – were the main fillers, along with the universal variations on the theme of minced-up meat: 'kotleti'. You could fill up further with stodgy, dry cakes and white, stale bread. (Much better, fresh, black bread is available from the shops.) The smetana (soured cream), by the large glass-full, seemed honest and nutritious, but the coffee was mostly dandelion by the taste, and pre-sugared. The whole lot came to less than 1 rouble – about £1 at official exchange rates.

This sort of meal may not seem like a tempting prospect, but one quickly develops a robust unfussiness about life's basic necessities. Better surely to eat in stolovayas, or queue up in the shops for bread and picnic ingredients, than be tied to having to return to the hotel for all your meals.

As a kind of complement to the somewhat stark, disinfected utilitarianism of the stolovayas, there exist the champagne-and-ice-cream parlour cafés. But alas! since Gorbachev began his Drive Against Alcoholism, these are no longer champagne-and-ice-cream parlours. Now they are lemonade-and-ice-cream parlours. These places, like the named restaurants, are subject to the problems resulting from the 'demand-exceeds-supply' situation, and so you may need to queue and/or wave foreign currency about, to get in. You may have no problems but if you do, remember that their soft, self-indulgent ambience, presided over by stern-looking 'babushkas' in grey overalls, is worth a bit of effort to savour. The ice-creams come in old-fashioned silver bowls, with the heavy, sticky, real flavours of fruit or chocolate smothering them. Since you've no choice but to squash up at the tables with strangers, they're good places for conversation practice. Most of the standard guide-books list these cafés – there aren't that many of them in Moscow and Leningrad. These are several on Gorky Ulitza, Leninskii Prospekt and Kalinin in the Arbat district.

there are in 1991!

In the other cities, eating seems to be less of a problem, and more enjoyable. The further south you go, the more fruit and vegetables (such as tomatoes) seem to be mentioned. This is hardly surprising as they grow more readily in the warmer climate. But everywhere, meat will dominate, often in extremely unappetising forms.

The simplest way to prevent hunger calling a halt to your wanderings is to take some snacky food with you. The best way is to get kidnapped by a Soviet citizen. Then, you may well get to sample home cooking. It won't always be lavish but it will be as far from Western 'junk food' as is possible: chicken will taste like chicken, eggs like eggs, you will almost certainly encounter the reassuring aroma of fried or boiled pototoes, and your friends may well go to the trouble and expense of trying to get hold of some of those rare and precious fresh vegetables for you. If cucumber and cabbage, spring onion and tomatoes *do* appear on the table, their freshness and full-bodied, earthy appearance will testify to their origin as being one of those assiduously cultivated strips of land that, looking from the train window or from your plane as it descends over the city's outskirts, you see behind each wooden village house.

ENTERTAINMENT: HOW TO GET SEATS AT THE THEATRE

Tickets for any interesting plays are always 'defitsinye' – in such short supply as to be officially unavailable. However, one seasoned visitor advises that the following strategy has never failed: 'Don't be deterred by the standard "nyet" at the box office. Ask to see the administrator ("administrator" in Russian), take your passport with you, literally beg him on your knees for a ticket as you are only here for such a short time and want to see the best in Soviet theatre, etc., and chances are he will give you a standing ticket.'

The reason this system works is that many tickets are always issued to various groups *en bloc*, and not all are used up. So for any function on any night, there are always some spare to be handed out at the last minute. Of course if *everybody* tried to do this, it wouldn't work any more . . .

It is always worth going along just before a 'sold-out'

performance of anything you're keen to see, in case there's a chance of a last-minute ticket.

USING YOUR TONGUE*

Even if you find no time before the journey, at least spend the flight learning the Russian alphabet, so that you can read the names of streets, Metro stations and so on. Our phrase section gives high priority to asking the way, but of course you'll need to exercise all the brain cells you can muster to decipher the directions that might ensue. Don't despair: remember the favourite Russian habit of accompanying you all or part of the way anyway. One contributor advises spending a day or two on the Moscow Metro as a way of absorbing the Cyrillic alphabet.

You may by now be wondering how all the fluent conversations recorded in some of the accounts in the first section of this book took place. Did all those visitors speak Russian? No, they didn't. What some of them did was to take a home-grown Russian-speaking guide with them. A 'trio', with one Russian-speaker and two who speak little or none, is a small enough group to be inconspicuous, and big enough to feel companionable. Once you get larger than that, you become an unwieldy size to fit around the Russian kitchen table, but more importantly, your opportunities for conversation, when everything has to be translated, become more limited. There are many Russian departments in British universities, and all will have students learning the language. Why not find the nearest source of Russian-speakers to you, and put up a notice asking if such a person might be interested to accompany you on a visit? There may well be plenty who would jump at the chance to have some exploratory-minded travelling companions.

WHAT SHALL I WEAR?

What you take to wear only really matters in the winter, since in

*See Appendix I (The Russian Alphabet) and II (Useful Phrases and Hints for Non-Russian Speakers)

the summer you can always take things off. But if you haven't got the gear to withstand the winter weather, fear of frostbite far from home can prove a disincentive to tramping the streets. Good quality down anoraks are the thing, but you'll be very noticeable. A lot of Russians wear fur coats, with many layers underneath. Lots of layers, trapping air in between, are always warmer than just one or two thick ones. The pavements are swept clear of snow usually, but the temperature can mean a good pair of boots making the difference between gaiety and misery. Winter visitors found thick, insulated snow boots were good. If there is a lot of snow, you'll need a pair of shoes for indoor wear so you won't drip melting sludge everwhere.

All buildings have huge cloakrooms: it is very bad manners to enter anywhere with your coat on – you leave it in the cloakroom. Interiors are very well heated. So you need somehow to combine clothes you won't be sweating in, with outdoor covering to cope with arctic cold.

You won't be able to go out at all if you don't have a hat, and one that has flaps to cover your ears or a knitted balaclava, and warm gloves, and a scarf you can use to cover your face. Modern fluffy acrylic things are hopeless – what you need is wool, that will at least keep some insulating power when it's covered in snow. Army surplus shops are good for cheap, solid, warm gear.

In the summer it gets very hot indeed, and mosquitos can be a problem. 'Take Anthisan, or similar, for insect bites,' writes one summer visitor. Western sanitary protection does not exist except as a black-market item in the USSR, so make sure you check dates and have ample supplies in case you need them.

USING THE PHONE

Public phone booths are to be found in central Moscow and outside large blocks of flats everywhere, although sometimes these are vandalised. (Soviet officials sometimes find it hard to understand why Westerners find that evidence that Soviet urban youth aren't too good to be true is reassuring instead of alarming.)

You need two one-kopeck pieces or a two-kopeck piece (*dvushka*, if you want to ask for change). First you place the coin in the slot, and then dial the number. When the connection is made, then the coin drops into the slot. There is a brief hesitation, and then you can talk. If you don't get through, keep trying, and remember the Soviet telephone system's phone 'ringing' and 'engaged' signals don't sound like ours. Also, many public phone booths don't work very well and your call doesn't always get through. We managed to make calls from public boxes, but sometimes if would take half an hour to achieve success.

There aren't any directories. There is a 'Directory Enquiries', but it is reputed to be permanently engaged. The number is 09 (it's called *Spravochnoye*) and you need the correct spelling of the last name and the patronymic of the person you want and, in some cases, their date of birth and address. Even if you've got those details, chances are you could be knocking on their door by the time you get their phone number.

ENTERING AND LEAVING

Entering and leaving the USSR can be rather intimidating. As you walk the corridors from the plane to the customs desk and passport control, small groups of officials scrutinise the new arrivals. The passport booths are manned by very young men in uniform. They stare at you for a long time – sometimes a full three minutes – before they are assured that you are indeed the bearer of the passport, and they sometimes ask sharp questions, such as why aren't you with your husband. Don't bother to try any flippancy – it's not their job to provide easy-going affability. Just stand it out.

Not everybody gets a customs search, and very few are body-searched or asked to turn out their pockets. You are less likely to be searched if you're with a delegation or a large party. We are sorry to report that people with Jewish-sounding surnames or Jewish appearance are more likely to be searched.

They are looking for literature, especially Bibles and any-thing written in Russian, such as addresses, undeclared money or valuables, excessive amounts of tradeable items (such as electronic ware indicating an intention of black market trading) and drugs, including prescription drugs such as antibiotics, in quantity. *DON'T* try taking any 'soft' drugs such as cannabis in with you. You won't need the extra stimulation anyway, and you really could end up with a heavy prison sentence.

Books about the Soviet Union, such as *The Russians* by Hedrick Smith, might be confiscated if found. However, the only way that Soviet people gain access to any perspective on their country other than that officially sanctioned, is through visitors who bring such materials with them. Single copies of religious books such as the Bible *can* be brought into the Soviet Union, since they are accepted as intended for personal use; but religious books in *Russian* may be confiscated.

It seems to be OK to take in food, even very perishable items like sausages. Unlike the passport men, the customs officials do engage in limited interaction, responding favourably to the discovery of stashes of peace literature, for example. They may sometimes decide, however, to treat themselves to small items, e.g. jewellery, that are obviously intended as gifts.

It is very important to give some thought to the question of *addresses*, on your way in or out of the country. If you are searched going in or out, addresses will be something the customs officials will be looking for – they do things like turn books upside down and flap them about to see if any little bits of paper fall out. Perhaps the simplest way to avoid your contact going on file is to memorise the addresses you want or directions for finding addresses and then, just to remind yourself, code them in English into your own address book or diary. Some people buy invisible ink pens from toy shops and use those, but the drawback to this method is that you need to take the pen with you so that you can rub over the invisible bit to reveal the writing – so if you lose your pen while over there, you're stuck. There really is no substitute for memory – after all, the Russians have had to learn to use their memories in the absence of readily available typewriters, photocopiers and so on – so why shouldn't we?

Make sure that all your film stock is in your pockets before you enter or leave the country, as Soviet X-ray machines will damage your films. (For other tips about photography see the 'Enemy Images' section.)

The first thing you will need to do on arrival is change some money. But most foreign currency desks at the airport close about 8.30 p.m. – even those that are meant to be open 24 hours. You need to show your customs declaration, which was stamped when you passed through customs. This is your first introduction to the huge importance accorded little bits of paper. You should keep all change receipts, since you might be asked to produce them when you leave, especially if you have changed too much and want to change roubles back into pounds or dollars. This is theoretically possible, but when I tried to do it the woman in the airport 'kasse' said she didn't have any sterling and could only offer me Deutschmarks. In return, I discovered that I'd thrown away all my vital change receipts, including the original customs declaration for how much money I'd brought in, and so we shrugged our shoulders at each other and called it quits.

The difficulty of changing money back into hard currency (and you're not allowed to take roubles out of the country – if they are found by customs, they'll be confiscated) means that it's best to change fairly small quantities at a time. Things are cheap, so £30 or £40 is plenty, especially if you have all your meals provided at the hotel, even if you plan on skipping some of them.

When you leave the country a search is highly likely if you have been skipping your programme and visiting people. Body-searches don't seem to happen unless, say, you've been on a non-stop round of visiting well-known dissidents still living in Moscow or Leningrad, or unless something the authorities regard as suspicious is found in your luggage – such as the wrong sort of book (e.g. this one). Searching someone's person involves bureaucracy, which is more work, so it's not under-taken that lightly, and there has to be some person, some 'peg' to hang the procedure on. If you have seen the Group for Trust or any other people in whom the KGB takes an interest then you should assume that you will be searched. This may or may not extend to having to turn out your pockets; occasionally someone is strip-searched but it's not usual.

Again, literature is a main object of the search: *samizdat* documents, letters, and diaries. It seems uncertain whether or not they have the right to confiscate material such as your lovingly kept diary. They can always photocopy things if they really want them, and it seems worth making a fuss (throwing a 'skandal') if they try to keep any of your property. A proper 'skandal' means complaining very loudly, pointing out how pointless and idiotic this kind of thing is, since it only alienates people who otherwise might have very pleasant things to say about their stay in the USSR. There seems little rhyme or reason to these searches, so you might as well stick to your guns if you think you're the victim of arbitrary unfairness. One traveller related how he had to negotiate with armed, jumpy Mongolian border guards on the Trans-Siberian, over a book of water-colour sketches of landscapes which they insisted on confiscating. He won in the end.

If you are leaving in a car or coach you may expect the vehicle to be treated to the kind of search British customs do when they're looking for heroin; and train compartments are gone through very thoroughly, often with dogs. This can include, and on the Trans-Siberian into China *does* include, virtually pulling the whole interior to bits.

Ann Pettit and Other Contributors
Trade Between People

'*It is a crime to arrive in Moscow empty-handed*' *(Aksyonov,* The Island of Crimea*)*

'*Thank heavens the world is full of petty law-breakers*' *(Fran De'ath)*

It is inevitable that the people one meets by the 'bumping into' method in the USSR may well be motivated in various ways to want to meet you. The commonest personal approach a Westerner may encounter is that of the 'fartsovchik' – the blackmarketeer.

The approach of the professional may easily be recognised and rebuffed; but not every person whose opening gambit is a query about items for sale, or who will ask you to do them a favour, is necessarily a hard-boiled professional. To one visitor, the distinction was clear.

In the subways and boulevards around Red Square, a discreet distance from the Hotels Moskva and Metropol, foreigners will inevitably encounter representatives of the so-called 'black-market'. This term, with its connotations of profit and deceit, is wholly inappropriate to describe an important section of the traders – a mainly teenage subculture whose devotees are determined enough to risk the authorities' disapproval and possible reprisals, in their quest for the paraphernalia of Western youth, with whom they wish to identify. For them items of clothing, such as fashionable T-shirts, labelled jeans and trainers, are in great demand, but of particular value are records and cassettes. In certain sections of Moscow youth, large groups will gather in the house of whoever has the sound system to sample the latest street acquisition.

Without exception, those I met who wished to buy goods were genuinely thirsty for experience of that which lies beyond the frontiers of their own culture – a perfectly natural desire in teenagers anywhere, which in our culture might normally be satisfied in foreign travel. Once talking, I found their knowledge of English music, magazines, cars and motorbikes and other aspects of our culture, quite astonishing. In many cases, here are true students of Western life, and their forays onto Moscow streets to meet with tourists and acquire what they could was, from this perspective, valuable field work. The trade was for them a kind of ritual bonding between East and West, with constant lament that our meetings had to be clandestine, and that they were unable to offer more by way of personal hospitality.

In contrast to this, I was stopped one afternoon on Kalinin Street, outside a bookshop, by a heavy-set, middle-aged man. He approached me from the doorway, wearing an outdated and flamboyant red nylon tracksuit, sporting the name 'Los Angeles' on the breast pocket. He had a scar above one eye, and he grinned whilst saying in heavily accented English, 'You want to buy roubles on black market?' My hackles rose immediately and choosing the path of ignorance, I replied, 'What do you mean black market?' 'You know black market, all tourist know black market,' he said, 'buy roubles, three for pound – you English?' His grin had turned into a leer. I moved on with a firm 'No thank you' and then I noticed him glance around to a man who was standing behind an open car door about 20 yards up the street, intently eyeing our exchange. I crossed the street, and watched the red tracksuit disappear back into the doorway, leaving me to draw my own conclusions.

You need to use your own judgement of character as to whether proffered friendship has a purely material motive; professionals are unlikely to bother very much with you if it becomes apparent you haven't 'trade' to offer and our accounts show that the 'black market' is so widespread that virtually the entire population must be involved at some level. Moreover, 'Trade' in a planned economy has many levels, as Fran De'ath found:

> The black market forms an enormous network. It's not just money and goods that are trade either but favours too. There are social favours which can include an introduction to a foreigner. I found that on making friends, a second meeting would always include several of their aquaintances. I definitely felt like a commodity. Not that I minded being part of a network; it meant that I could meet a wide range of people – singers, engineers, even a Komsomol leader (Youth Party).
>
> What intrigued me about this network was that within a rigid, totalitarian system, a whole culture flourished based on trust. These people didn't necessarily like one another, but the system created an interdependence. Mutual co-operation I have found to be the rarest quality in a group of people and here it was ticking over very nicely via the black market with its tendrils gently around most of the population of Leningrad.

To understand why this is such a tricky, grey area we need to briefly revisit square one: we must look again at the factors arising from the differences between the way 'their' society and 'our' society are run, and the barriers that exist.

A basic asymmetry is created by the Soviet restriction on access to the West for its citizens, and many tensions that shape personal contact flow from this. A kind of 'restricted zone' is thus created and only certain people are meant to inhabit it, for it is a region of both privilege and, from the point of view of a Kremlin 'hard-liner', danger, from spies and contaminating

ideas. Approved access to this Western-inhabited zone, with its
opportunities for obtaining all manner of 'defitsinye' (scarce,
sought-after) goods, and the highest value commodity of all –
information – is limited and therefore desirable.

The result is that when you as a Westerner arrive in the
Soviet Union, to vast numbers of Russians everything about
you has the glow of forbidden fruits. *Everything* – not simply
your access via the hard currency shop in your hotel to goods,
such as popular books or, nowadays, vodka unavailable in the
rouble shops outside – but your conversation, your ideas, your
experience of the world, even your knowledge of the Soviet
Union itself – will be the object of someone's desire.

To some extent, the Intourist 'cocoon' protects the visitor
from the disturbing effects of exposure to these tensions. The
doorman in the hotel, for instance, is partly there to prevent the
'fartsovchiki' reaching you. On the other hand, he or some of
the other 'insiders' may naturally be keen to corner their own
little piece of the trade, and want to exclude any competition.

This visitor followed advice given by a party of Italians in the
hotel to trade currency with hotel staff rather than in the street,
on grounds that you're less likely to get fleeced as you'll see
them again.

After registering, I got into the lift where there was a young
porter, with his trolley. He immediately asked if I would like
to change money. I've never been one to dip my toe in first –
so I plunged. 'Yes.' My friend, Annie, was grimacing at me
'Don't be daft' and shrinking back in the corner. While I
haggled over the rate, up and down we went. Others entered
and left as we did our bargaining in hasty moments when we
were alone in the lift. I settled for three roubles to the pound;
he rolled up my £10 and put them in the tubular steel of his
trolley a bit grudgingly – he wanted me to change a larger
sum.

On leaving the country, you have to fill out a money form,
but it's easy to account for the missing sterling as the hotel
bars only accept this for their over-priced booze. As it turned
out it wasn't necessary for me to lie anyway.

It would be wrong, however, to depict all hotel staff you might encounter as rapacious devourers of Western goodies. Some, such as the floor-ladies to whom you have to hand in your key when you leave, may be well-used to giving favours, like making you a cup of tea when you arrive in the middle of the night. It would be churlish not to reward them with a gift, but it's safe to assume that they see plenty of the action in the way of tights, soaps, cosmetics and so on. But the humbler workers who are more 'behind the scenes' – the kitchen ladies, the cleaners and so on – responded with tremendous warmth, tinged with surprise, to our packages. The lady cleaning our room gave me such a bear-hug she nearly squashed the breath out of me, and looking at her over-worked, knobbly legs I felt really glad to have given her a nice pair of attractive, warm, tights for the winter. In return, she let us leave our bags in the room after we had officially checked out of it, thus saving us a lot of hassle taking them across town to the station left-luggage.

As with many other areas of Soviet life, it is hard to discern what is exactly illegal, what is tolerated and what is perfectly legal and allowed. Masha Davies comments:

One of the funniest episodes was being pursued by a huge Georgian gentleman in a rusty old lorry, who kept on stopping behind us, rushing out of his cab to enquire about our willingness to sell jeans, jackets, blouses, in fact anything 'modern', preferably with a 'Levi' label attached to it. Each time we beamed our middle-aged smiles at him, revealing our appalling lack of trendy Western clothes, yet he continued his campaign, undeterred. At the last imminent 'hi-jack' – we had in fact been stopped by a routine police check – the Georgian rushed out of his cab with his 'spiel', pushing the Russian bobby out of the way. Far from angry, the policeman was highly amused and only after about five minutes of the Georgian 'pleading' did he cheerfully intervene, urging him to stop nagging 'pristavats' – nice tourists – like us. All this was accompanied by much laughter and slapping of shoulders, and not the slightest acknowledgement of the absurdity of the situation.

The cheerful acceptance by the policeman of open black marketeering in Georgia reflects the impression given by others who have stayed in the Georgian capital, Tbilisi. It would appear that 'trading' is so embedded in the Georgian and Armenian characters that no amount of state control has been able to eradicate it. Many 'story-jokes' abound to illustrate this theme. As if finally bowing to the inevitable, some limited 'economic reforms' have been allowed in Georgia, begun when Shevardnadze, Gorbachev's new foreign minister, was the region's boss. These include private ownership of some restaurants, and a form of workers' co-operative ownership of the bus service. This does not mean that all Georgians are only interested in Westerners from a material point of view – see section on 'Brief Encounters, Friends and Lovers'.

Although currency transactions are apparently very common and for all we know the majority of visitors change money in this way and come to no harm, we can't advocate this method of cutting one's costs! Those that *are* caught risk prosecution for committing a 'Crime Against the State', for which the penalty is 3–8 years imprisonment. The Foreign Office have no record of anyone British being penalised in recent years, but point out that KGB attempts at blackmail are the most likely result for someone who gets caught, so they probably wouldn't end up in court.

But even at official rates of exchange, prices for food and public transport are very cheap compared with our own, so the risk of 'doing deals' with a complete stranger may not be worth it. Even if all that happens is that those caught get swiftly booted out of the country, their time in police custody is likely to be rather nerve-racking, as they wonder whether they are going to experience a more prolonged stay than they had anticipated.

If you decide beforehand that you are going to be good and not take part in trading, this doesn't mean that you can float airily above the sordid material world of *things*. Don't get too hoity-toity if you're asked to do 'favours' by people – remember it is very humiliating for Soviet people to have to beg Western visitors to buy them things from the Beriozki shops they cannot enter, even though it is their country. It may be illegal to trade, but there's no law against giving. If you do make friends with someone who's happy to be your 'informal guide' it is likely anyway that they will want to pay for you, and if you're invited into a home, you'll be fed with as many treats as can be rustled up. A visitor will feel the need to reciprocate. Generosity can be the way out of the dilemma of wanting to do someone a requested favour, while not wanting to do anything illegal.

Even the most fleeting encounters can sometimes be marked by amazing, embarrassing generosity, as the following anecdote from Masha Davies' storehouse of stories well illustrates:

In Smolensk I visited the newly refurbished magnificent cathedral. I started chatting to one of the old ladies, dressed in black, who busy themselves with cleaning, the lighting and selling of candles, etc. inside the church. I mentioned that I was Orthodox, whereupon the old lady looked sternly at me and shrieked: 'Oh no, you can't be . . .' On seeing my bewildered expression, she said a little more softly: 'Where's your cross then?' I instinctively groped round my neck and answered rather apologetically: 'Well, you see, we had a burglary at home . . .' The little babushka looked at me even more sternly and then disappeared behind some icons. Seconds later she emerged and very quickly and furtively she wound something around my neck and with a big, broad smile she announced: '*Now* you are a proper Russian Orthodox. God bless you!' Only someone who realises the scarcity of gold jewellery in the Soviet Union can appreciate the enormity of this gift of a gold cross and chain. She would not accept a kopek, and to this day I can see this cross-looking lady's transformation to a beatifically smiling saint-like figure.

So it is worth giving some time and thought, and seeking advice, about the suitability of a selection of gifts. To the Westerner educated in the current left-liberal tradition, the whole area of gift-giving is a moral minefield. To my mind, however, it is sheer cowardice to try to avoid the whole problem by just taking over a bagful of peace badges and a few biros. The question must be confronted: What would I like to give and what would they like to receive? The two may not add up to the same thing.

For example, there is no doubt that packs of make-up, such as those delicious-looking boxes of lipsticks and nail varnishes on sale in well-known Western chainstores, make enthusiastically received gifts. But the preparation of my last visit found me hovering like a dragon-fly around the counter laden with what I knew to be most delectable selection of goodies, although I had long since grown bored with their empty promises. Is it right to indulge Natasha's illusions about Western glamour? Shouldn't I get her a good book instead?

But if you do arrive with nothing but Greenham photo-essays in hand, you may find yourself feeling suddenly rather mean. Russian women often make painstaking efforts to beautify themselves and their surroundings in the midst of what appears to be a brutally harsh landscape. Why shouldn't Natasha want to decorate herself and her flat?

Evidently I was not the only one to suffer the pangs resulting from this particular piece of paradoxical fence-sitting:

> I had no qualms about changing money, although I did feel moralistic about taking jeans and stuff like that to sell as I don't do that kind of thing at home and saw no reason why I should indulge in selling goods abroad. Although I had nothing to trade anyway, I did change my attitude about this as well. I shamefacedly realised that city dwellers in Russia are very European. There were plenty of clothes in the shops, but they were lacking style. I don't think that I am a victim of consumerism, and I admire the lack of pre-packaging of goods in Russia, but I do find that I enjoy clothes and the degree of self-expression through them, so I could hardly decry the want in others.

We know that the West's glamourous image is simply packaging. It seems wrong, somehow, to foster an illusion about our society by flashing nicely finished goods. But on the other hand, we take it for granted that most of the everyday things we deem necessary for existence in an industrial society are there on sale. It is hard for us to appreciate the frustration of everyday life – especially for women – when even things like soap powder, and shoes that fit have to be assiduously hunted down, let alone the things almost impossible to find like Tampax, contraceptives or disposable nappies. One tends to agree with the comment that, 'Given the lack of these domestic appliances and public services, the development of consumer goods production is a feminist issue in the Soviet context.'*

There is a thin line between fostering illusions about life in the 'consumer society' and foisting moral humbug about materialism upon the Russians we meet. And finally, where does all that Western currency end up? Fran De'ath remarks:

Before I went to Russia, I read an assortment of books on the country and there was invariably a section on the black market but none had tackled the question of what they *do* with foreign currency. It must be a vital link in the supply of goods like hi-fi systems; things that the moralisers at home have in abundance.

Everyone I met seemed to have plenty of roubles in the pocket, but that won't fill your flat with music or buy a calculator. For those you need hard currency, connections or both. As the rouble is not exchangeable, toe-lining party members who get to travel abroad need hard currency, and I wouldn't be surprised if some of it found itself into their pockets and fluttered eventually into a till at Marks and Spencers.

SUGGESTIONS FOR GIFT-GIVING

This section, like the previous ones, has been compiled from the results of a questionnaire sent to British visitors to the USSR, and with the kind assistance of a number of people with

*Quoted from 'The New Soviet Woman: Model or Myth?' Change Report No. 3.

a greater familiarity with Soviet society, who have lived there or visited frequently.

One of the simplest things to take is a Western newspaper. It is relatively common to find Russians who speak, or are learning, English – far more common than the reverse – and the Russians who are interested in ideas relish the chance to have access to an alternative source of information.

Take the *Sun*! We met some Russian students of English and the only English language paper they ever saw was the *Morning Star*. We only had the *Guardian* with us (how typical). It's the first time I've ever wanted a copy of the *Sun*.

Best of all, take a selection of the papers on sale the day you leave – if a common language can be found, you have the ingredients for many hours of fascinating discussion.

Small 'tokens of friendship' are good to give friendly taxi-drivers, hotel staff, anybody you meet at random. Such things might be: postcards of Britain or art reproduction postcards, nice pens and biros, little note-books and diaries, jewellery, badges for collection-obsessed children and grown-ups, tights, soaps, Tampax, razor-blades, cigarettes and children's toys like plasticine and toy cars.

If you have hopes of being given impromptu hospitality, you will feel awful if you don't have anything with which to acknowledge a host's generosity. Highly prized passports to conversation include instant coffee ('Campaign Coffee' from Tanzania is not only ideologically 'sound' but is also light, as it comes in a plastic bag), exotic teas, biscuits, salami from your local delicatessen counter, nuts, pickles, chocolate, anything you can add to the 'treats' that will be put before you. An unusual, cheap and lighweight gift, guaranteed to delight, would be a selection of *spices*, e.g. nutmeg, cinnamon, vanilla pods, curry spices, peppercorns, ginger. It may seem absurd to take vodka to Russia but the Gorbachev Drive Against Alcoholism has struck hard at traditional Russian hospitality. Some people may actually be inhibited from inviting you into their houses because they can no longer provide the customary bottle of vodka. But you can – from your Beriozka, or better still, from the duty-free shop at the airport before you leave.

If you know particular people there before setting out, then you will want to take them more substantial gifts and need to give careful thought as to what will please them the most. Some would be delighted by clothes, others would be terribly disappointed if you missed the opportunity to bring in some coveted books (see note on 'Literature' below) while yet others might be thrilled with some wizard electronics. But a word of warning! One of our contributors tells the sad story of a digital watch whose workings were so complicated the thing proved useless. Don't forget that batteries are hard to get, and that anything needing frequent injections of know-how or spare parts might also prove a back-hander.

One way to give certain delight – and something that should never be forgotten when visiting a family – is gifts for the children. Almost anything will be welcome, including little picture books, baby clothes, nappies, toys . . .

Clothing

Levi's, who now base their advertising upon their reputation as the commonest Soviet 'alternative' currency, no longer open doors and oil wheels the way they used to, apparently. In the trouser line, it seems corduroy is more desired. Anything that's well made and fashionable will be welcome, including natural-fibre dress material and particularly real wool (not acrylic), knitting needles and knitting and dress patterns. A contributor writes:

> The bottom is dropping out of the jeans market, though even the home-grown variety still cost over 100 roubles in the shops. You might get 30 roubles for your old Levi's but it's probably not worth the effort of sneaking off to some grotty stairwell to display your wares every time a new bunch of high school capitalists accosts you on the street. If you want to make a few roubles then take in sweatshirts, T-shirts or jackets with western logos. £9.99 Woolies trainers will fetch 30 roubles with no problem but it's less easy to explain the

presence of 25 pairs of shoes than 24 T-shirts if your luggage is searched on your way in. And don't forget that there is very little worth buying in the shops in roubles anyway.

Literature
One person who is a frequent visitor writes:

> Take quite a few books and magazines for people you meet. You should avoid material which is identifiably 'anti-Soviet' and will therefore be confiscated by customs – e.g. works by Orwell, Trotsky, Solzhenitsyn – and also anything that might count as pornographic, which will also be seized by the customs officers [we don't know if this applies to the *Sun* or not. We await reports . . .] But you can take through many publications which are of interest to Soviet people and not widely available in the USSR, while not being 'anti-Soviet': British fiction, peace and ecology literature, literature about Third World problems (such as *New Internationalist* magazine) and many other topics. Celebrity, royalty and fashion magazines are also very popular.

Don't forget that much of the literature on sale in the Beriozki shops may be like gold-dust in the street outside. The same writer adds:

> As well as getting souvenirs for yourself remember that many of the things make excellent gifts for Soviet friends, such as books by Bulgakov, or the rural writers Shukshin, Astafayer, Abramov, Pasternak, Akhamatova, and Mandel'stam. It is nice to give a present to your guide also.

To this I would add that recently published novels and poetry in Russian may be available in a Russian bookshop like Collet's, Charing Cross Road in London, while practically unavailable in the Soviet Union. I've never seen a book so eagerly or rapidly devoured as a collection of poems by the late popular balladeer, the Russian Bob Dylan-figure, Vysotsky. It lay there, ignored on its Western shelf. But the face of the

Leningrad sociology student who was the lucky recipient lit up
with joy when he saw the cover. 'This book is published here,'
he said, 'but nowhere can you find a copy. They must publish
just a few thousand and then send them all abroad.'

Even copies of the classics of Russian literature – works by
Tolstoy, Chekhov, Pushkin, Dostoyevsky and so on may be
'defitsiniye'* and much easier to find, in the Russian language,
in Collet's bookshop here. Such a gift would always be
welcome, because even if the recipient already had the book, it
would have barter value.

It is common-sense to point out that if your bags are filled up
with leaflets of any kind that look as if they are meant for
distribution, you will be regarded as a threat to State Security,
and the same applies to copies of the Bible.

Music

Many visitors report interrogations by Soviet youth whom they
meet informally, on the subject of current Western music
trends. When they can't reel off that week's Top Twenty they
feel they've let their listeners down. There's so much going on
here, and there's so much eagerness for it there, that lists of
suitable tapes and records likely to please are irrelevant and you
might as well rely on your own preferences. And if you can't
make up your mind, Beatles or Jazz classics tapes would always
go down a treat with someone. Blank cassettes are compact and
useful as well, since much of the music produced by Soviet
semi-licit groups circulates via endless copying of tapes.

Pushkin Square in the centre of Moscow is reputedly a
meeting-place for traders of tapes and records of Western
music, but such places also attract the attentions of the KGB so
caution would be advised. Why not take a small tape-recorder,
so that you can bring back some tapes of Russian rock or jazz
music. Recent reports suggest that some very exciting things are
happening musically and that the Soviet 'underground' rock
scene is mushrooming.

If you're uneasy about participating in what may seem to be a
one-sided form of 'cultural exchange', the following quote from

*'difitsiniye' – whatever is sought after, scarce or unobtainable at the time.

a recent magazine article about the Russian punk/rock music
scene may reassure you:

> Western music is vital not because we are blind imitators but
> because we cannot create something new without exchanging
> ideas.*

Finally don't overlook the usefulness of the personal photo
album as a useful bridge to communication. One respondent to
the questionnaire writes:

> I took a scrap-book showing photos of my family, town,
> peace group, etc. It was invaluable for getting into conversa-
> tion and people were really interested. Other more imagina-
> tive friends took pictures showing bad housing, urban decay,
> the seamy side of Western affluence, just to counter the
> impression that it's paradise here.

What to Bring Back

Beriozkas have some nice painted toys, though the carved
animals and Matryoshka dolls are fairly exhorbitant. Elsewhere
try the large bookshops where a marvellous range of art and
political cards can be found for only 2 or 3 kopeks each. Also
posters can be bought very cheaply. In most large cities there
are artists' shops which sell original works in many media –
always a bargain. In artist materials shops you can also usually
buy a good range of quality, signed lithographs, screenprints
and etchings for between 3 and 6 roubles, and that includes a
frame with glass. Stationary shops have nice odds and ends at
very low prices, e.g. the ubiquitous abacus for just a rouble or
two depending on size.

   The most stimulating 'trade between people' is in ideas. One
person states simply:

> What to bring back? – Friendship – sorry to sound corny but
> it's true.

*The *Observer*, 'Back in the USSR', 4 August 1985.

Books

FOR ARMCHAIR SLAVOPHILES

Most of the Western correspondents from the English-speaking countries have, on their return from their stint in Moscow, written books about their experience. These books form the easiest introduction to the nature of the Soviet system and the way it affects people's lives. The classic and most useful of this genre is still *The Russians*, by Hedrick Smith. Others in the same readable, anecodotal style include *Russia: The Power and the People* by Kaiser and *Russia Perceived* by Elisabeth Pond (which has a Trans-Siberian travelogue thrown in as well). More recent are *Russia: Broken Idols, Solemn Dreams* by Shipler and *Life in Russia* by Michael Binyon, although Shipler was more adventurous as a correspondent and hence his book is more interesting. All these books record the landscape of what has come to be known as the Brezhnev Era. The essential features of the Soviet system such as these books describe remain today but two more up-to-date, general introductions to the Soviet scene are *The Working Light* by Martin Walker of the *Guardian* and *Letters from Moscow* by Richard Owen (*The Times*). Since they both cover the years from Chernenko to Gorbachev from different viewpoints they make a good pair. Richard Owen's book is in the anecodotal, vignette style; Martin Walker's book is more of an analysis of Soviet society at the dawning of the Gorbachev era.

Some travel writers have attempted to capture the elusive quality of the USSR's atmosphere. The travel writer Colin Thubron has written a book recording his journey by car along those routes where Intourist will permit you to venture. *Among The Russians*, published in 1983, was recommended to me by several people. I found it an honest, but rather gloomy, account. He does meet plenty of people, including the KGB, for he comes in for the suspicion that seems to dog any lone Westerner in the USSR, especially those with occupations deemed euphemisms for spying, such as 'writer', 'journalist' and so on. For anyone intending to follow in Masha Davies' footsteps, this book is a must.

Likewise Eric Newby's *The Big Red Train Ride* is a good primer for would-be travellers on the Trans-Siberian, although if you read Elisabeth Pond's book (see above) you get more social commentary and more of the general experience of a correspondent with your impressionistic travelogue.*

The views of the correspondents are necessarily shaped by the suspicion which surrounds them, and this limits their access to people and to some extent defines their relationships: it is very hard for them to meet or make friends with 'ordinary people'. The exchange student is somewhat freer in this respect, and Andrea Lee's little book *Russian Journal* (Faber) reflects the good use a curious and acute observer made of this freedom. Her book is simply a collection of stories describing the people she got to know, and for a good read that's a tantalising introduction to 'life on the other side' I'd recommend this book as a Best Buy.

I found that the more I read about the Soviet Union and discussed it with others who'd recently been 'hooked', the more I wanted to find out. Of course, there is no more hotly contested subject than the history of the USSR. It is worth trying to get hold of an early official Soviet version of the post-revolutionary state of affairs, just to get an earful of the language by which the Bolshevik rulers have chosen to describe themselves. I'm lucky enough to have inherited a *History of the CPSU, 1936* which is invaluable, not as source of fact, but as an example of the distortion produced at the height of the Stalin era. A young sociology student I met in Leningrad asked me if I could bring him an 'objective' history of the Russian Revolution. I find it touching, now, that he should assume that such a thing exists, somewhere.

Two books available in paperback are: *The Russian Revolution and the Origins of Present-day Communism* by Shapiro, and *The Making of the Soviet System* by Moshe Lewin; another work recommended by a lecturer in Soviet history, since it deals

---

*Portrait of all the Russians by Laurens van der Post is an ambitious attempt to capture the many cultures and landscapes of the Soviet continent. The text is compelling and the photos rivetting. Anyone going on the Central Asian tours should read this.

with both pre- and post-revolutionary Russia is *Russia: the Roots of Confrontation* by Robert Daniels, Harvard University Press.

Roy Medvedev's *Khrushchev* is fascinating reading, as is the more recent study of Andropov by Roy's twin brother Zhores, who lives in this country. Zhores was quick off the mark with his *Gorbachev*, published by Blackwell in 1986. Another recent history is *Gorbachev: The Path to Power* by Christian Schmide-Haver. It is Roy Medvedev also who sat up in the middle of the night painstakingly documenting the 'crimes of the Cult of Personality' which resulted in his mammoth work, *Let History Judge* – another vital work you won't find in 'The World's Largest Bookshop' on Kalinin Prospekt.

The hallmark of the Medvedev brothers is a painstaking attention to accuracy; it is truth they're after, and they know how sloppy scholarship can be used by the forces ranged against them to discredit the entire effort to chronicle the events of the world's greatest social experiment. That is why Roy Medvedev wrote *Let History Judge*, as an effort to record, as factually and truthfully as possible, those events for which Solzhenitsyn relied on anecdote – three huge volumes' worth of them – in *The Gulag Archepelago*. Not everyone in the Soviet dissident scene agrees which Solzhenitsyn's analysis of his country's problems, and his proferred solution, but few can dispute that he is a damn good writer, and any newcomer to Russian studies can hardly pass by his classics, *One Day in the Life of Ivan Denisovitch*, *First Circle* and *Cancer Ward*, as well as his short stories. A recently published biography of Solzhenitzyn by Michael Scammel is available in paperback and would make a good introduction not only to the man but to his times as well.

If you want a picture-book to introduce you to pre-revolutionary Russian history, you could try *My Russia* by Peter Ustinov, and if you want to know who Bukharin was, or if you want to know *anything* that could be called a fact, look it up in *The Cambridge Encyclopaedia of the Soviet Union* – there should be one in your library. If you want to keep regularly informed about Soviet developments from an 'objective' standpoint, a new magazine called *Détente* aims to bridge the gap between professional sovietologists and the interested amateur. Available from Collet's or Dr Jeff Gleisner, Dept of Politics, University of Leeds.

The habit developed by the Soviet State of booting its best writers Westwards, has given us access to a whole range of works dealing with the unmentionable other side of the coin of official optimism. As casually as we can flip through Solzhenitsyn on a station bookstall, we can also turn the pages of Voinovitch's delicious satires (*The Life and Times of Private Ivan Chonkin* or *The Ivankiad*) or try to comprehend the incredible Swiftian excesses of Aleksander Zinoviev's vast edifice of irony, *The Yawning Heights*. We can, at our leisure, digest and discuss any of the classics of *samizdat* published in the West – an excellent collection might be the edited selections from an underground bulletin compiled by Roy Medvedev from October '64 to March '71. It's called *An End to Silence: Uncensored Opinion in the Soviet Union*, edited by Stephen Cohen.* We can read those revered poets, Akhmatova and Mandel'stam, in full and uncut versions (the Writers' and Readers' copy of Mandel'stam, translated by David Mcduff, has the original Russian as well, so it's good for language learners) and we can read Nadezhda Mandel'stam's stunning recollection of the life of a poet in those most lethal times, *Hope Against Hope*. And of course we've no difficulty getting hold of Pasternak's poems.

It is a terrible irony itself that we, who can read the latest 'forbidden' works, are scarcely interested in the raging debates, while the jokes and allusions of the novelists are all too often lost on our reading public. However one book I found glued to my hand until I'd finished it was Aksyonov's *The Burn*. It was like a literary helter-skelter around the Moscow of the sixties and the Siberia of the early fifties, passages of exhilarating parody and wild farce alternate with sobering descriptions of the author's experiences as a young boy sharing his mother's exile in Magadan after her fifteen years in prison camp. Her

---

*Not to mention the scholarly analyses, by ex-Soviet academics such as Yanov, Turchim and Zaslavsky, of contemporary society.

name was Eugenia Ginzburg and her memoirs *Within the Whirlwind* are themselves a classic of 'prison camp literature' written with tremendous sympathy, humanity and humour. My only reservation about *The Burn* is that it reflects the world of the solipsistic male who manages to describe sex without the question of contraceptives, let alone foetuses, coming into it at all.

On the whole, the female voice is conspicuous by its absence from modern Russian writing. Two volumes of feminist *samizdat* exist, published by Sheba, called *Women and Russia*, and Allison and Busby have published a collection of interviews privately conducted with a range of women by two Swedish women journalists, Hanson and Lidell, entitled *Moscow Women*. All of this is thought-provoking reading. After all, we campaign here for what they've supposedly 'got' over there in the way of the socialisation of child-care and wonderful maternity conditions and equal pay for equal work . . .

Virago, I notice, have just begun to publish a few fiction titles by contemporary Russian women writers who are sufficiently within the fold to be published in their own country. It will be interesting to see what insights these writers give us into the predicament of Soviet women, for the questions raised by that predicament are relevant for us, too.

Finally there is the question of guide-books themselves. *The Blue Guide to Moscow and Leningrad* is recommended by one visitor, who says the maps are good. Fodor's guide is up-to-date and comprehensive. A new book *Coping With Russia* by Robert Daglish, has plenty of know-how, but is more geared to the needs of the long-termers such as diplomats, correspondents or business people taking up residence, than the visitor. For fun and brutal honesty and an insight into the Soviet alcoholic scene (which must by now be well underground as the Drive Against Alcoholism recreates the atmosphere of the Prohibition) try Polonsky's *The USSR: From an Original Idea by Karl Marx*, published in 1986 by Faber.

Ann Pettitt
Post-Chernobyl Postscript

Most of this book was written before the Soviet nuclear reactor at Chernobyl in the Ukraine blew up, scattering about ten per cent of its radioactive atoms over a huge area of the Ukraine, Byelorussia, Finland, Scandinavia and the rest of Europe. Chernobyl has provided a bitter education into the dangers of nuclear power; it is not within the scope of this book to say any more than that about the wider and long-term implications of this event. But it has created, like nuclear waste, a number of new problems and practical questions for the traveller which will not easily be answered or disposed of.

The main question is this: 'Will I expose myself to an increase in radiation dose if I travel to the USSR?' Subsidiary questions are: 'Is it safe to go to Kiev or Byelorussia?' and 'What about the food? How can we tell if it's contaminated or not?'

The first, general question is more easily dealt with than the specific ones. By now, many of the radionuclides, particularly the iodines, have decayed away. By the time this book is being read, the only significant problem remaining will be caesium 137. Because of the way the wind carried the radioactive plume, parts of Scandinavia and also Britain received far higher doses on the ground, where rain brought down the particles, than much of European Russia and particularly Moscow. So food grown in the Moscow area is likely to be carrying less caesium than food grown in much of the rest of Europe. Judging by where the radiation was carried, Copenhagen, Warsaw, or Stockholm and our own Lake District are still more radioactive as a result of Chernobyl than Moscow. But Leningrad and its surrounding area was in the path of the plume. However, as it is a city, much of the radioactive caesium will by now have been washed off the concrete and stone surfaces by rain.

The Foreign Office updated its advice to travellers concerning the health risks on the 3rd November 1986. They now say that there are no risks arising from radiation to short-term travellers to any part of the USSR, including the Ukraine and Byelorussia, the areas which received the highest fallout. They base this statement on tests carried out by the NRPB on foodstuffs on sale in the USSR, which show that food contaminated by radiation above levels considered 'safe' in this country, is not being offered for sale in the USSR either. They do say, however, that travellers should heed 'any advice they hear', but stress that there is no danger from food officially on sale. By 'short-term' they mean up to six weeks. People staying longer than that, says the Foreign Office, will gradually accumulate an increased dose of radiation: but they say this is likely to be still within the limits considered acceptable for workers in the nuclear industry.

In assessing the relative risk of travel to the USSR, it is worth bearing in mind the following general point about radiation. Those most at risk of damage, mainly of developing cancer, are first of all those whose bodies are growing fastest, and secondly those whose bodies are ageing. The fastest growing creatures of all are the unborn ones, followed in descending order by babies, children and teenagers. Adults in their prime are the least likely to suffer long-term harm from radiation. As people become older, so they become more susceptible. The official Russian figures for post-Chernobyl radiation levels in ground, water and air in the Moscow region show no significant increase above the normal.

Appendices

Printed		Written		Pronounced approximately as in the English	
А	а	*А а*		a	in 'father'
Б	б	*Б б*		b	in 'book'
В	в	*В в*		v	in 'vote'
Г	г	*Г г*		g	in 'good'
Д	д	*Д д*		d	in 'day'
Е	е	*Е е*		ye	in 'yes'
Ё	ё	*Ё ё*		yo	in 'yonder'
Ж	ж	*Ж ж*		s	in 'pleasure'
З	з	*З з*		z,s	in 'zone', 'easy'
И	и	*И и*		ee	in 'meet'
Й	й	*Й й*		y	in 'boy'
К	к	*К к*		k	in 'kind'
Л	л	*Л л*		l	in 'bell', 'belt'
М	м	*М м*		m	in 'man'
Н	н	*Н н*		n	in 'note'
О	о	*О о*		o	in 'port'
П	п	*П п*		p	in 'pen'
Р	р	*Р р*		r	in 'ride'
С	с	*С с*		s	in 'sister'
Т	т	*Т т*		t	in 'it'
У	у	*У у*		oo	in 'book'
Ф	ф	*Ф ф*		f	in 'five'
Х	х	*Х х*		h	in 'hut'
Ц	ц	*Ц ц*		tz	in 'quartz'
Ч	ч	*Ч ч*		ch	in 'lunch'
Ш	ш	*Ш ш*		sh	in 'short'
Щ	щ	*Щ щ*		sti	in 'question'
	ъ		*ъ*	('hard sign')	
	ы		*ы*	i	in 'bill'
	ь		*ь*	('soft sign')	
Э	э	*Э э*		e	in 'men'
Ю	ю	*Ю ю*		u	in 'use'
Я	я	*Я я*		ya	in 'yard'

Appendix II

Useful Phrases and Hints for Non-Russian Speakers.

Some recognition of the Cyrillic alphabet is important, particularly when travelling on the Metro. It is quite important to know the difference between **ВЫХОД** and **ВХОД**. Words like **ТУАЛЕТ** ought to be recognizable.

Bring a pad and a pen, as well as plenty of miming and body-language. Try saying the words in English – they might just be similar, e.g. taksi, telefon, etc.

Very basic vocabulary:

da and nyet	– yes and no
ya nye znayoo	– I don't know
zdrá(v)stvuyte	– hello
da svidánye	– goodbye
spasíba	– thank you
pazhálsta	– don't mention it, please, sorry!, help yourself
náda	– it is necessary (important), I (he, she, etc.) must
mozhno?	– is it all right, allowed? – may I borrow (have) . . .?

da, právilyno	– yes, that's right
právda	– yes, you are right, that's correct
mozhno sigaryetu/zakoorit'?	– may I have a cigarette – may I smoke?
nekultoorna	– 'not done' (e.g. leaving one's coat on in cafés, museums, etc.)
harashó	– fine, all right
nýeharasho/plóha	– bad
kak harasho	– how nice
kak vkoosna	– tastes delicious (how delicious!)
izvinitye	– so sorry! – apologies! (didn't hear you – pardon? pazhalsta? can be used in the same way)
kak	– how?
kak viy	– how are you?
gdye	– where (is) (are)?
pachemóo	– why?
pachemóo nyet	– why not?
kto éta	– who is it?
kagdá	– when
inagdá	– sometimes
vsyegdá	– always

Asking and understanding simple directions:
izvinitye, ya nye gavaryoo pa rooski – sorry, I don't speak Russian
ya nye panimayoo – I don't understand
izvinítye (skazhíte pazhálsta) – état avtóbus/póyezd yédet v . . .?
– tell me please – does this bus/train go to . . .?
pamagítye nam (mnye) pazhálsta – help us (me) please.
miy hatím (ya hachóo) paití v . . . – we (I) want to go to . . .
gastínitsoo (normally gastinitsa) – hotel
stántsioo – station
éta myesta – this place
état ádryes – this address
miy nye znáyem gdye miy/miy zablyoodílis – we do not know where we are/we have got lost
kak daití da . . .? – how do I get to . . .?

da, padazhítye – yes, just wait a second
nyet, eta nye vash avtóbus – no, this is not your bus
moźhna nam/mnye pakazát . . .? – can you show us/me . . .?
pakazhíte pazhálsta – show me please
gdye . . . Metró/kaf'é/restorán/muzéy – where is/are . . .
Metro/café/restaurant/museum?

Introducing yourself:
menyá zavoót . . . my name is . . .
kak vas zavoót? – what's your name?
ya zdyes' (toot) adnoó nedélyoo – I am here for a week
miy – we
dva/tri dnyá – (two/three days)
chetírye   – four
pyat'   – five
shest'   – six
sem'   – seven
vósyem   – eight
dyévyat'   – nine
dyésyat'   – ten
viy   – (polite) you
tiy   – (familiar) you
on   – he
 aná   – she
 aní   – they

Getting into conversation:
gdye viy zhivyotye/tiy zhivyósh'? – where do you live?
ya (zhivóo) v gastínitse Metropol – I live/stay at hotel Metropol
ya angliski tourist – English tourist
ya iz Lóndona – I'm from London
ya/miy iz Ánglii, Amériki, Austrálii – I/we are from England,
America, Australia
ya otdiyhaýoo (oo menyá ótpoosk) – I am on holiday
ya hachoó vstrétit' rooskikh – I want to meet Russians
ya hachoó ooznát' kak róoskiye zhivóot – I want to find out
how Russians live
ya ne gavaryóo pa-rooski, ya gavaryóo pa frantsoóti/

pa nemyetski – I don't speak Russian, I speak French/German
ya rabótayoo v shkólye – I work in school (mime your job)/
bibliatyéke – in the library/dóma – at home
ya zarabátayoo éta v nedéloo/za mésyats – I earn this in a
week/month
éta ya dalzhná trátit' – this is what I have to spend
mayá lyoobiḿaya moózyka . . . – my favourite music/groópa
. . . – group
ya óchen' lyooblyoó . . . – I like . . . very much
ya nye lyooblyoó – I don't like
viy lyóobite – do you like?
viy sliyshali pra . . .? – I have you heard of . . .?

Photos:

vot mai déti	– my children
mayá dóchka	– my daughter
moi syn	– son
mayá máma	– mother
moi pápa	– father
moi moozh	– husband
mayá zhená	– wife
moi brat	– brother
moi droog	– boyfriend
mayá padroóga	– girlfriend

ya zhivoó v górodye – I live in town/v derýevnye – in the country
vstrétimsya apyát', da? – shall we meet again
Vstrétimsya apyát', da? – let's meet again
sevódyna? – today?
sevódnya dnyóm? – this afternoon?
sevódyna vyecherom? – this evening?
závtra? – tomorrow?
tó zhe myésta? – the same place?
váshe myésta? – your place?
oo Metró? – by the Metro?
toot (zdyes') – here?
nye toot (zdyes') – not here
ya nye magóo – I can't manage it
náda ití – I/we have to go

zhalka! – what a shame!

ya tat ráda [1] vas vstrétit' – I'm so glad to meet you

gróopa – general, magic word – cheap (sometimes even free!) entrances and dinners

Rather basic needs:

ya hachoó yest' – I am hungry (lit. I want to eat)/thirsty

ya óostala [2] – I am tired

gdye tooalyét? – where is the toilet/is there a bath?

gdye vánnaya? – where is the bath?

mnye plóha – I'm feeling sick/not well

dóktar pazhálsta? – could I/we get a doctor please?

biýstra – quickly

Food and shopping:

gdye mózhna pakoóshat'? – where can one get something to eat?

mózhna koopít' – where can one buy . . .?

hlyeb	– bread
máala	– butter
eyr	– cheese
frookty	– fruit
vadá	– water
minerál'naya vadá	– mineral water
sok	– juice
malakó	– milk
smetána	– sour cream
myása	– meat
salát	– salad
marózhenoye	– ice-cream
chai	– tea
kófye	– coffee
kefír	– yoghurt-like liquid
lozhka	– spoon

---

[1] *rada* is the feminine form; *rad* is masculine.
[2] *óostala* is feminine; the masculine is *oostal*.

vílka   – fork
nózh   – knife
cháshka   – cup
stakán   – glass
chai/kôfye/byez/sákhara   – cup of tea/coffee without sugar

gdye kássa – where is the till?
daitye mnye pazhálsta? – can I please have . . .?
skol'ka stoit? – how much does it cost?
éta óchered' shtóby koopít'? – is the queue for buying?
éta óchered' platit' – is this queue for paying?
éta vsyó – that's all
gdye póchta? tri marki v angliyoo – where is the post office? –
three stamps for England. (Add *avia* and it might get to
England *before* you!)

Other useful words and phrases:
Droózhba myézhdoo západom i vastókom – friendship between East and West
miy vse hatím mir – we all want peace
oo nas tózhe problyémy na vastókye – we have problems in the
West too
kanyéshno, vsyo mózhna koopít', no vsyo tózhe dóroga – sure,
we can buy anything, but life is expensive . . .
niktó nye pabedít yádernooyo voinóo – no one will win a
nuclear war
gosoodárstva – government
palítiki – politicians
lyóodi – people
déti – children
nóviy mir – a new world
prastáya zhizn' – ordinary life
zhizn' tróodnaya – life is hard/netróodnaya – easy
zhénshchiny – women
mooshchíny – men
dóma – at home
rabóta – work

Dealing with unwanted approaches:
Nyet, nichevó – no – we have nothing
idíti – go away
oobiráityes' – get lost!
nye pristaváiti – don't keep on (nagging)
brós'te – leave off!

Making a fuss (last resort):
éta oozhásna! – that's appalling
gloópa – stupid
miy váshi gósti – we are your guests
toot vsyo tak priyátna a éta vsyo ispórtila – it has been lovely,
but this has spoiled it all

Collet's International Bookshop (129–131 Charing Cross Rd,
London WC2 0EQ) sells a good selection of suitable phrase
and guide books and dictionaries.